Feng Shui Your Own Home

With the 9 Steps to Feng Shui® System

Monica P. Castaneda

Feng Shui is the ancient Chinese Art of Placement and has been in use throughout the Orient for thousands of years. The complex wisdom of the Feng Shui aspects gathered in these pages constitutes the dynamic experience of the author. An investigation of these inspired words is meant to lead you to your own understanding of this complex wisdom. The author makes no claim for absolute effectiveness. The adoption and application of the advice or information offered is solely the readers' responsibility. The author of this book does not dispense medical or psychological advice or prescribe the use of any technique as a form of treatment for medical or mental problems without the advice of a physician, either directly or indirectly. The intent of the author is only to offer information of a general nature to help readers in their quest for spiritual wellbeing. If the reader chooses to use any of the information in this book as is the reader's constitutional right, the author assumes no responsibility for the reader's actions.

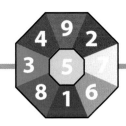

The Chinese say:

First, **Luck**

Second, **Destiny**

Third, **Feng Shui**

Fourth, **Virtues**

Fifth, Education

Feng Shui, the ancient art of placement,
was designed thousands of years ago to help
people create the conditions that can make
it easier to live a good life.

Feng Shui uses the laws of nature to determine "what to put where" so you can: Feel More Relaxed, **Get Along with Others Better, Be More Productive,** and **Attract Greater Abundance.**

Feng Shui draws knowledge from Nature and Universal Laws in order to produce environments that promote Wealth, Health, Love and Happiness.

Feng Shui proposes arranging the space in order to reproduce the signs of nature that we recognize as **life-nurturing and safe.** This provides us with positive feedback about our lives.

Feng Shui can help you create a home or work environment where you can feel **safe**, in greater **harmony** with your surroundings and in better **control** of your spaces.

"Feng Shui" means Wind and Water

The term "Feng Shui means literally "Wind and Water" the forces that shape the landscape. It is pronounced "Fung Schway" and it refers to a set of rules in Chinese philosophy that govern spatial arrangement and orientation in relation to patterns related to the Universal Laws, as expressed in the Natural World.

It is said that the term Feng Shui is actually a short way to refer to an ancient poem, which described the ideal conditions of a place where human life could thrive, in harmony with Heaven and Earth.

> The winds are mild,
> The sun is bright,
> The water is clear,
> The trees are lush.

Feng Shui is at least 5,000 years old. The Feng Shui masters of Ancient China had the responsibility of finding sites where palaces, farms, and villages could be built with a certain guarantee that people could not only survive, but prosper there. They also were to find burial sites where the memory of ancestors could be honored for generations. At a time when there were no weather reports and history had just started to be recorded, Feng Shui practitioners had to rely on their powers of observation of the natural world.

In modern times Feng Shui also deals with the surroundings of a building [including streets and other buildings], its shape and landscaping, as well as with the colors and materials of the outside and inside of a space.

Feng Shui Your Own Home offers you the opportunity to utilize the knowledge of Feng Shui without having to devote a lot of time to study.

"A loving atmosphere in your home is the foundation for your LIFE. Do all you can to create a tranquil, harmonious home."

(Taken from the *Instructions for Life*, Author Unknown)

Table of Contents

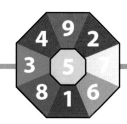

Feng Shui Your Own Home: Key #1

Please answer the questions and follow the instruction in the corresponding sections of the book in the order they are presented. As you complete chores, come back to this key and address the next question.

1. Is the floor plan of your home complete? A complete floor plan is square or rectangular, with no missing parts. U shaped, C shaped, L shaped and irregularly shaped floor plans are considered incomplete.
☐ Yes   Skip to chapter 2
☐ No   Go to chapter 1 and learn how to complete your floor plan

2. Does your home have a long and narrow hallway?
☐ Yes   Go to item 2.1
☐ No   Go to the next question

3. Are there any ceilings in your home that are too low or too high?
☐ Yes   Go to item # 2.2
☐ No   Go to the next question

4. Are there any rooms in your home that are too small or too big?
☐ Yes   Go to item # 2.3
☐ No   Go to the next question

5. Are any rooms in your home too dark or too light?
☐ Yes   Go to item # 2.4
☐ No   Go to the next question

6. Now go to item #2.5 and see if you are dealing with any of the problems listed there. When you are done, go to the next question.

7. Read page 22 and the top of page 23 , then go to the next question.

8. Do you and others get a good impression when arriving at your place? Whether your answer is yes or no, check out ways to increase curb appeal in item #3.1.1

9. Do you have any trees blocking the entrance or trees blocking windows?
☐　Yes　　Go to item #3.1.2
☐　No　　Go to the next question

10. Do you see something beautiful as soon as you walk in your house?
☐　Yes　　Go to the next question
☐　No　　Go to item # 3.1.3

11. If you would like to learn how to enhance your foyer go to item #3.1.4

12. Do you know what items attract good chi, in other words items that are chi magnets?
☐　Yes　　Go to the next question
☐　No　　Go to item # 3.1.5

13. Go to item #3.1.6 and take a look at the conditions of an ideal Feng Shui entrance and compare this with the main entrance to your home. Then answer these questions:

What parts of the ideal entrance are already present in your entrance?

_____

_____

_____

What parts of the ideal entrance are missing in your entrance?

What actions could you take to bring your entrance closer to the Feng Shui ideal?

----

14. Does your front door face a door to the outside or a large window?
☐ Yes   Go to item #3.2.1
☐ No   Go to the next question

15. Are there any straight paths inside or outside your home?
☐ Yes   For straight paths inside your home go to item #3.2.2
           For straight paths outside your home look at the side bar
           on page 22
☐ No   Go to the next question

16. Does your home have ceiling fans?
☐ Yes   Go to item #3.2.4
☐ No   Go to the next question

17. Are there any staircases in your home?
☐ Yes   Go to item #3.2.5. If your staircase faces the main door go to
           item #3.2.5.1
☐ No   Go to the next question

18. Are there any walls creating sharp angles at the corner?
☐ Yes   Go to item #3.2.6
☐ No   Go to the next question

19. Are there any exposed beams inside your home?
- ☐ Yes   Go to item #3.2.7
- ☐ No   Go to the next question

20. Are there any corners of other buildings or roofs pointing directly at your front door?
- ☐ Yes   Go to item #3.2.8
- ☐ No   Go to the next question

21. Is your home located on a corner lot?
- ☐ Yes   Go to item #3.2.9
- ☐ No   Go to the next question

22. Go to item #3.3 to learn how to prevent chi (life force) stagnation and drains.

23. Are there a lot of windows in your home?
- ☐ Yes   Go to item #3.3.5
- ☐ No   Go to the next question

24. Do you have any room with strange angles inside (not 90°)?
- ☐ Yes   Go to item #3.4.1
- ☐ No   Go to the next question

25. Are there any walls in your home that are not completely vertical?
- ☐ Yes   Go to item #3.4.2
- ☐ No   Go to the next question

When you are done with question number 25 move on to Key #2, on page 36.

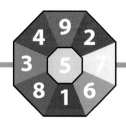

Feng Shui Your Own Home

Step

Complete the Floor Plan

In Feng Shui we consider a floor plan complete
when it is a full square or rectangle.

A complete floor plan helps you connect with the idea
that you have been given everything you need to live
a life that is happy, healthy, prosperous and free.

Incomplete floor plans need to be completed.
Turn the page to find out how.

STEP ONE: COMPLETING THE FLOOR PLAN

The first thing you check a house for is completeness. Does its perimeter, when seen from above, form a complete square, a rectangle (most common), oval, circle, or octagon? If it doesn't, say, if your floor plan has an L, C or U shape, it has to be fixed. The cure to apply here is either physically or virtually to "complete" the building.

Whenever possible, apply cures both on the inside and on the outside.

1.1 FROM THE INSIDE

- To cure an incomplete shape from the inside, we use **stained glass**, semitransparent **curtains**, **mirrors** or pieces of **artwork** that have a long distance **perspective**.

  - We use **stained glass** or semitransparent **curtains** when there are windows present.

  - We use **mirrors** to create the visual impression that the space continues into the area that is missing.

  - We use **paintings** of landscapes seen from afar (long distance perspective) whenever it is not practical to use mirrors.

  - We place items that will soften the sharpness of the edges generated by the incompleteness (or "missing" portion of the perimeter) on the inside. For example, strings of beads, cords and tassels, mobiles (except wind chimes, which should only be used outside or by a window that stays open most of the time), plants, round tables with pots or flower arrangements on top.

A corner is missing in this home, at the far back of the living room. To complete the floor plan, a large mirror has been placed on one side of the missing area, and sheer curtains have been used for a window on the other side of the missing area.

A large plant has been added in front of the corner to cover it up.

If you don't want to or cannot use a large mirror, you can also place a painting of a landscape with long distance perspective, that is, an image with very small items on it so they look like they are far away. It doesn't have to be as large as what you see in the picture above, but enough to give you that depth perception.

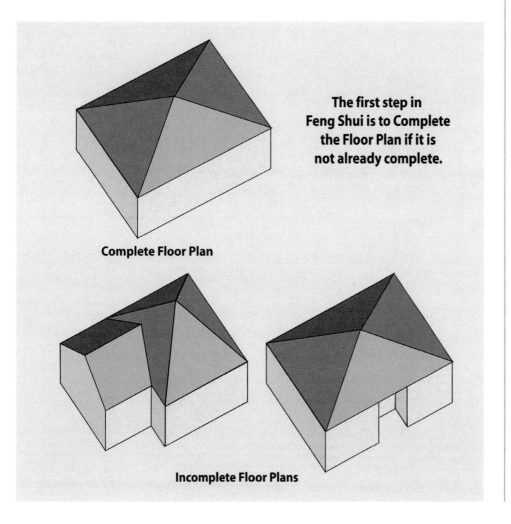

Complete Floor Plan

The first step in Feng Shui is to Complete the Floor Plan if it is not already complete.

Incomplete Floor Plans

1.2 FROM THE OUTSIDE

- To cure an incomplete building from the outside we can either **fill** it **in**, draw an **outline** or **mark** the **corner**.

1.2.1 FILL-IN THE MISSING AREA

We can **fill in** the missing area with a flower bed, tiling or gravel (to make a patio).

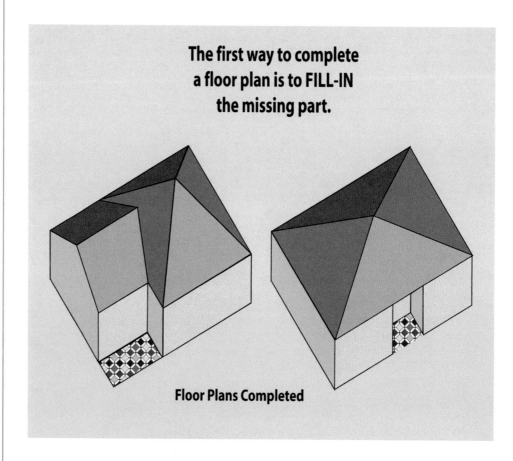

The first way to complete a floor plan is to FILL-IN the missing part.

Floor Plans Completed

IDEAS TO FILL IN THE MISSING AREA:

- Tile
- Gravel
- Landscaping Stones
- Cement patio
- Flower bed

1.2.2 DRAWING A LINE AROUND THE MISSING AREA

We can **draw** an outline to complete the portion that is missing. Drawing the line only on one side, and leaving the other side open, works too, or even just suggesting a line by placing items at intervals (as if it was a dotted line) on what would be the perimeter of the building if it was a complete shape.

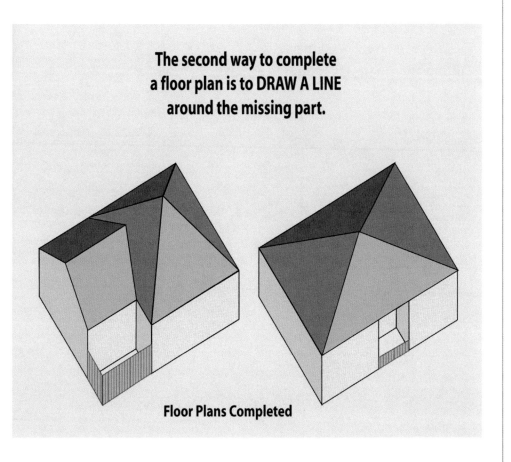

The second way to complete a floor plan is to DRAW A LINE around the missing part.

Floor Plans Completed

IDEAS DRAW THE LINE AROUND THE MISSING AREA:

- Fence
- Hedges
- Landscaping edging
- Line of stones
- Line of flowers

1.2.3 MARKING THE CORNER OF THE MISSING AREA

We can **mark** the corner at the point where the projections of the two sides of the building would meet if the home was a complete shape (square or rectangle).

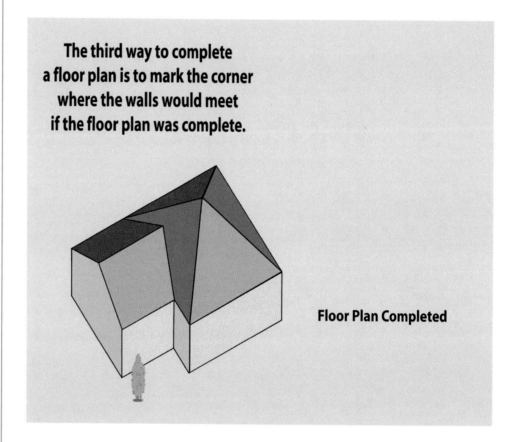

The third way to complete a floor plan is to mark the corner where the walls would meet if the floor plan was complete.

Floor Plan Completed

IDEAS TO MARK THE CORNER OF THE MISSING AREA:

- Small tree or bush
- Potted plant
- Flag
- Light post
- Shepherds hook
- Quartz crystal planted with the tip up, the tip being about one inch under the topsoil.

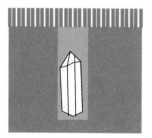

What size should a piece of natural quartz crystal be to cure a missing corner?

Use this formula: 2" long for every 1,000 sq. ft. on the floor located at street level, then add 0.5" for every additional story.

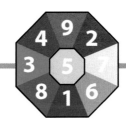

Feng Shui Your Own Home

Step

Balance Extremes

An extreme is anything in the building that you could describe as "too much" or "too little" or "too" anything.

The very fact you look for the word "too" in order to refer to anything in your home indicates that there is an imbalance.

In Feng Shui we use opposites to "cure" or fix imbalances.

It is a common mistake in interior decor to place a mirror at the end of a hallway. This makes the hallway twice as long, exacerbating the problem.

A bright painting or poster with large images is a better choice for the wall at the end of the hallway.

Placing a mirror on the side of the hallway is very auspicious (of good omen) because it makes the hallway seem twice as wide.

STEP TWO: BALANCING EXTREMES

Think opposites. Opposites attract. The reason they attract is that they are trying to balance each other out: hot and cold; dark and light; narrow and wide; high and low; etc.

But how do you apply this in Feng Shui? The key is asking the question: **What is there too much/too little of here?** And then balancing it out with its opposite. The most common cases in a home are:

2.1 HALLWAYS
2.1.1 THE HALLWAY IS TOO LONG

> *Solution:* **shorten it**. You can shorten a hallway or corridor by:

- Placing mirrors, artwork and light fixtures at intervals, like in a zigzag pattern, to create points of interest.

- Placing something big at the end of the hallway, like a big vase with a huge floral arrangement or artwork with very bright colors, strong strokes and big elements painted on it. (Do NOT place a mirror at the end of a long hallway, or you will double its length).

2.1.2 THE HALLWAY (OR OTHER SPACE) IS TOO NARROW

> *Solution:* **widen it up**. You can widen up a room, a hallway or corridor by:

- Placing a mirror on one side.

- Placing artwork with long-distance perspective on one or both side walls.

2.2 CEILING HEIGHT
2.2.1 THE CEILING IS TOO HIGH

> *Solution:* you **lower it down**. You can lower a ceiling down by:

- Pasting a horizontal wall paper border at the height of eight feet from the floor.

- Hanging tapestry or flags from the ceiling to a height that feels comfortable.

- Hanging light fixtures and ceiling fans at a height where you can turn them on and off from the chain just by stretching your arm.

2.2.2 THE CEILING IS TOO LOW.

Solution: **lift it up**. You can lift a ceiling up by:

- Painting it in white or a pastel color.

- Placing light fixtures that point the light up. (Spot lights and uplighters)

- Choosing beds, chairs, tables, that are lower than standard (as in Japanese furniture), or placing cushions on the floor (Arab or Hindu style).

2.3 ROOM SIZE
2.3.1 THE ROOM IS TOO SMALL OR FEELS CROWDED

Solution: you **enlarge it**. You can enlarge the room by:

- Placing a big mirror in one wall, to visually "double" the size of the room.
- Placing artwork with long-distance perspective.
- Using furniture that is smaller than standard.
- Painting/decorating it with light colors.

2.3.2 THE ROOM FEELS TOO BIG, NOT COZY.

Solution: you **shrink** it. You can make a room feel smaller by:

- Painting it in rich tones (more proportion of pigment in the paint than white), like terra-cotta, or hunter green, what are now called "accent" colors.
- Placing big, bulky furniture to fill it up, (like most antiques).
- Dividing it up in smaller areas, where different activities are promoted. (For example: sleeping area and reading area in a big master room; or watching TV and conversation/games area in a big living room)

2.4 LIGHT AND DARK
2.4.1. THE ROOM IS TOO DARK.

Solution: you **lighten it up**. You can lighten up a room by:

- Adding lamps or other light fixtures, with at least one high wattage bulb in the room.

For high ceilings hang artwork with the top at the same height as the windows or doors, place light fixtures low, choose lamps that direct the light down, choose a ceiling color that is not too bright, and favor wall colors and window treatments in rich tones (saturated colors).

For low ceilings choose lamps and light fixtures that direct the light up, light colored or sheer window treatments, and make sure that ceiling is painted in a light color or white.

Landscapes or other artwork with long distance perspective help create depth in narrow spaces.

19

- Painting it with bright, light colors.
- Placing lively artwork, with bright colors and sunny themes.
- Choosing light colored furniture and draperies, but keeping the latter open whenever possible.

2.4.2 THERE ARE TOO MANY WINDOWS, TOO MUCH LIGHT/SUN COMING IN.

Solution: darken the room up. You can darken a room up by:

- Using furniture made of dark wood.
- Adding curtains and blinds.
- Decorating in dark tones.
- Placing tall plants or hanging plants in front of the windows. (See also item 3.5)

2.5 OTHER YIN/YANG ISSUES

Here are some other random examples of how you can use the yin and yang to create balance and harmony of the opposing forces yin and yang in Feng Shui:

Too humid –> dry it out with heat, light, and objects related to the earth element (earth absorbs water).

Too fragmented –> unify it, repetition of the same colors, themes and accessories in the different rooms of a house or office building that lacks uniformity can help create a feeling of unity. You can also use red tones (this color represents adherence, gluing things together).

Too cold –> warm it up, with light fixtures, tapestries, cozy furniture and warm colors (yellows, oranges, reds, browns).

Too old –> renew it, by redoing the walls, fixing whatever needs to be fixed, adding a couple of new items to the room or house.

Too old fashioned –> modernize it. Spicing up a room with a few whimsical adornments here and there can bring new life to an old style house or room.

Too cheap –> add value to it. You can do this of course by adding expensive or expensive-looking ornaments, but also with home-made adornments or with objects from nature that are elegant in themselves.

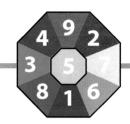

Feng Shui Your Own Home

Step

Optimize Circulation

In Feng Shui we seek a healthy circulation of air,
a smooth circulation of traffic and especially,
a vibrant circulation of CHI (the Life Force)

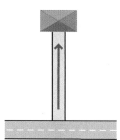

Straight pathways channel chi too quickly.

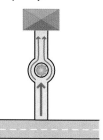

Inserting a circular shape into the pathway and directing the flow around a plant or water feature can slow down the chi.

Placing semicircular flower beds along the way creates the impression of a meandering path.

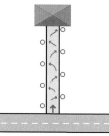

Low height light fixtures placed in a zig-zag pattern help slow down the chi, but they shouldn't be right on the edge, or they could become tripping hazards.

STEP THREE: OPTIMIZE CHI CIRCULATION

Chi is a Chinese term translated as "Life Force." Most people cannot see chi but most can be trained to feel it in their hands in less than one minute. If you have ever done yoga, tai chi, or belly dancing you probably have felt a warm, tingling, magnetic sensation in your fingertips. You were perceiving chi, the life force.

To better understand chi we compare it to things we know, like the wind, water flowing, light, sound and children.

• Beneficial chi moves in a slow meandering way, like a soft breeze.

• Chi can stagnate, like water, if it stops moving. When chi flowing alongside two walls meets at the corner, it creates turbulence, like when two rivers meet.

• Chi is a more subtle energy than light, so anything that produces an effect on light also produces an effect on chi.

• Chi is absorbed by porous surfaces and bounces off smooth surfaces, like sound.

• Chi is attracted by anything that would attract a toddler, and is sent away by anything that would scare a toddler.

There are three main principles of Chi:

- Where there is Life there is Chi
- Chi connects everything
- Chi is in constant motion, producing changes as it moves

THREE KINDS OF CHI

Beneficial chi - bright, meandering chi.

Cutting chi - chi that moves too fast.

Stagnant chi - not enough chi or decayed chi.

WHAT TO DO TO HAVE HEALTHY CHI

In order to achieve a healthy circulation of the Life Force you need to:

1. Invite and collect beneficial chi
2. Slow down/ disperse destructive chi
3. Stir up stagnant chi, prevent chi drainage

3.1 ATTRACTING BENEFICIAL CHI

3.1.1 CURB APPEAL

1. Curb appeals starts with your mailbox. Make sure that the numbers are in good condition and clearly visible from both sides.

2. If the entrance to your driveway is far from the main door to the building, create matching landscaping features on both sides of the driveway.

3. Feng Shui correct paths are meandering, with soft curves. Straight pathways need to be worked on:

   - Use plants and garden elements to visually alter the shape of the path to a more curvy one (see sidebar on page 22).
   - Place light features or bright colored elements in a zigzag pattern.
   - If the path is wide enough you can slow down the rapid flow by placing beautiful garden art, vegetation or even a water feature halfway along the path (the direction of the water flow should be towards the house).

3.1.2 DEAL WITH TREES BLOCKING THE ENTRANCE

When a big tree is blocking the view from the street to the main entrance of a house or office building, it does not only prevent the entry of chi into the space, but it also may be preventing sunlight from coming in, producing a condition of excess yin.

Sad as it is, the best solution is to have the tree removed. Today, however, removing a tree does not necessarily mean letting it die, as it can be transplanted to another area of the same property or to a business property or city park.

Do some landscaping around the mailbox.

Mark your entrance by doing the same kind of landscaping on each side of the driveway.

A tree blocking the entrance is bad Feng Shui, but whenever you take down a tree, plant another four trees of the same kind (or have someone plant them for you).

If a tree trunk is not directly in front of the main door but the limbs and/or foliage are covering part of the door and windows...

... it can be pruned to allow for more visibility.

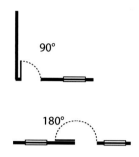

The door must open without obstructions to the full extent allowed by the walls, either 90° or 180°.

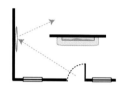

If the first sight after you open the main door is a wall, place artwork with depth, such as a landscape. If possible hang a mirror on a side wall in a position that will allow you to see the area behind the first wall.

If for any reason the tree must remain, you can have it pruned to reduce its foliage or the extension of its branches, to make the entrance more visible and let more light in. There are other things you can do, like painting the door in a bright color, or placing bright colored object by the entrance and hanging a wind chime of a rather loud but pleasant sound (not so loud that it will annoy you, though).

3.1.3 WHEN YOU OPEN THE DOOR

It is very important that when you first come in the door your attention is attracted to something beautiful, uplifting and peaceful. This applies both to your front door and your door from the garage, driveway or back porch.

3.1.4 OTHER TIPS FOR THE FOYER

- Have a generous non-skid rug on the floor right as you open the door; upgrade your current entry rug; alternate two rugs in the year, one for spring and summer and one for fall and winter.
- Place either a non-beveled mirror [wall that makes an L with front door] or a painting/poster with perspective [wall parallel to front door] in your foyer. Or better yet, have both! Even better, put these in luxurious frames.
- Place an entry table underneath the mirror or beautiful painting/poster in your foyer. Better yet, get a luxurious entry table.
- On your entry table you need to have a representation of each of the five elements (water, wood, fire, earth and metal), to do this place on your table top:
  - your choice of either a tall lamp and a low plant/flower arrangement, or short lamp, tall plant/flower arrangement.
  - **plus**: something yellow if the table top is metal, glass or marble; something red if the table top is wooden.
- Hang coats and hats, place umbrellas and boots in a place that is hidden [behind the doors of a closet] or half hidden.
- Have a good source of light overhead.

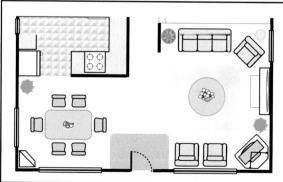

When the main door opens directly into a room, or in between two rooms or into an open concept area it is necessary to define a foyer, either by changing the kind of flooring around the door (usually tiles or vinyl) or by placing an area rug. This serves two purposes: protecting the carpet or wooden floors from dirt and mud from the outside, and creating a virtual transition between the entrance and the rooms.

- Make sure the entry table in your foyer either has rounded corners or is in the shape of a half oval and that the legs don't protrude in a way that might make someone trip.
- When you can, upgrade the flooring on your foyer for a more luxurious first impression.
- Place a small sculpture or antique trinket on the shelf underneath the table or a suitable ornament on the floor [something designed to be on the floor].

3.1.5 CHI MAGNETS EVERYWHERE

There should be at least one chi attractor right outside and right inside your main entrance. There should also be chi attractors distributed around the home and inside the home, to keep the energy up. Remember that chi is attracted to the same things that get the attention of a child.

ANYTHING THAT WOULD ATTRACT THE ATTENTION OF A CHILD IS A CHI MAGNET

NINE CHI MAGNETS
Water
Sounds
Living beings
Things that move
Light
Things that shine
Art
Nature
Bright, colorful objects

3.1.6 THE IDEAL ENTRANCE

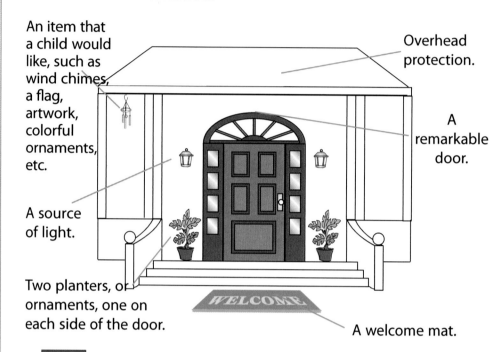

An item that a child would like, such as wind chimes, a flag, artwork, colorful ornaments, etc.

Overhead protection.

A remarkable door.

A source of light.

Two planters, or ornaments, one on each side of the door.

A welcome mat.

The most important elements of a good entrance are the "guards" on the side of the door.

There is always something you can do to transform an ordinary door into a remarkable door. Though the traditional color for doors in Feng Shui is the color red, this is not a requirement, as long as the door is clearly noticeable.

3.2 SLOWING DOWN OR DISPERSING DESTRUCTIVE CHI

Listed below are the most common chi problems found in homes:

3.2.1 A COMMON CHI CIRCULATION PROBLEM: DOOR FACING DOOR OR DOOR FACING WINDOW

When the front and back door face each other chi tends to escape too quickly, without visiting all of the house or room.

Hang an object that can gather and disperse chi like a 40 mm cut crystal sphere, a crystal lamp, a mobile (except wind chimes, these are only recommended outdoors or next to a window that is opened often) or any light fixture that sends the light out in a radial way, like the sun.

When two doors or a door and a big window face each other, the chi escapes too quickly.

Try any of these solutions:

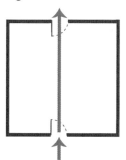

Hang a 40 - 50 mm faceted crystal ball from the ceiling midway between the two doors or between the door and window.

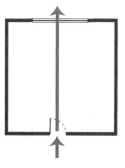

Cover up the window with a curtain in bright colors.

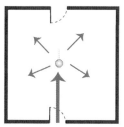

Place a round or oval piece of furniture in the way, with a nice flower arrangement or sculpture on top.

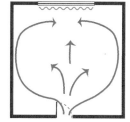

Hang plants in front of the window.

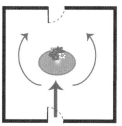

Place a beautiful screen to separate the area into two.

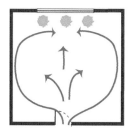

Hang a beautiful piece of stained glass (with smooth, non angular designs) in front of the window

In a long and narrow hallway people and chi tend to speed. Mirrors and landscape artwork placed in zig zag help create points of interest along the way.

Placing artwork and mirrors alongside a long corridor helps to slow down the chi.

Clear Faceted Crystal Balls are used in Feng Shui for Chi Corrections

3.2.2 STRAIGHT PATHWAYS: RACE TRACKS FOR CHI

Straight pathways produce excessive speeding of chi. Fast chi is not auspicious (auspicious means "of good omen").

- Place interesting artwork and mirrors in a zig zag pattern along the walls to slow chi down.

- Hang a 30-40 mm faceted crystal ball from the ceiling towards the center of the hallway to grab and disperse chi.

- Use light fixtures that disperse the light outwards, like those shaped like a plate.

3.2.3 FACETED CRYSTAL BALLS

The faceted crystal ball used in Feng Shui has nothing to do with divination. It is simply a **round** prism.

Faceted crystal balls are used in Feng Shui for several purposes:

- Hanging from the ceiling at the end of a staircase to lessen the feeling of "falling down."

- To create a point of interest in long hallways and to grab and redistribute chi, especially when the front and back doors are lined up with each other.

- As chain-pulls for ceiling fans.

- As a buffer when chi that is too strong is pointing directly at a person when seated or sleeping.

- To disperse "negative" chi

- As a reminder of your intentions when or while other fixes are not feasible.

Faceted crystals balls — rounded prisms — are very beautiful and reflect the light in different colors.

As a precaution, do not hang crystals by a window that gets direct sunlight.

3.2.4 CEILING FANS

These are made of "blades." If possible, hang them high enough so that the tallest member of your family cannot touch them with their arms extended.

Hang a pretty, flashy, fancy chain-pull from the chain. My favorite is a 30 mm faceted crystal ball, because it is a prism and anything that has the ability to redirect light can also redirect chi.

3.2.5 STAIRCASES

Staircases are considered "waterfalls of chi." For this reason, Feng Shui favors one-story homes.

Staircases with a landing are better than those with no landing. Straight staircases are better than circular stairs, both for safety reasons and because the latter produce a drain of chi.

3.2.5.1 WHEN THE MAIN DOOR FACES A STAIRCASE

This situation always poses a Feng Shui problem. If the staircase goes up from the foyer, this is a home where people tend to feel tired. A faceted crystal ball hanging from the ceiling resolves this situation.

If the staircase goes down from the foyer, this is a home where things seem to be "going down." In addition to a faceted crystal ball hanging from the ceiling I recommend a small gate at the top of the stairs.

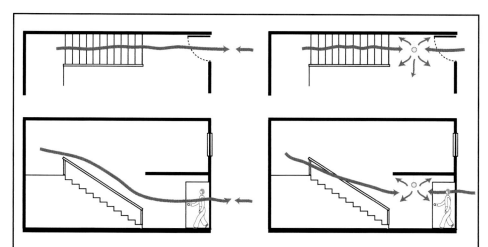

When a staircase faces a door that leads to the outside, chi speeding down the stairs will exit too quickly through the door and prevent fresh chi from coming in. You can hang a 40 mm faceted crystal ball from the ceiling halfway between the lower step and the door, in order to grab, slow down and redistribute chi in all directions.

The faceted crystal ball can also be used for staircases going down or for split foyers. In the case of a staircase going down, it is best if there is a closed door or a gate where the steps start to go down, or paint/stain the top step in a bright color. In the case of split foyers, place a bright rug on the side of the steps that leads to the more public areas of the home (living room dining room kitchen, etc).

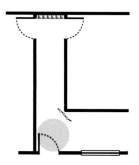

If the door opens directly into a hallway, place a round or oval rug near the door and hang bright colored artwork at the end of the hallway if possible.

If there is a corner pointing at the entrance, you can hang a string of beads from the ceiling to cover it up and soften the flow of chi.

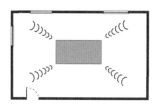

Sharp cornered furniture also sends turbulent energy into a room...

... choose furniture with rounded or beveled corners to avoid this.

A corner cured by placing a large plant in front of it.

A split foyer is related to indecision. Hang a crystal ball right above the spot where the railing starts, and place a bright rug in front of the flight of stairs that goes up.

3.2.6 "SHARS": POISON ARROWS

Chi meets at the outside of corners and speeds up in the direction pointed by the "arrowhead" formed where the two walls meet (when seen in the floor plan, see graphic below) in destructive ways. This "arrowheads" are known as "shars" or "poison arrows" in Feng Shui, and can occur both inside and outside a building

- Physically soften the shape of the corner, either by beveling the point, or making it rounded, if this is possible, it solves the problem for good.

- Hide the corner with plants, flags, water features, strings of beads, tassels, or any other ingenious idea of yours.

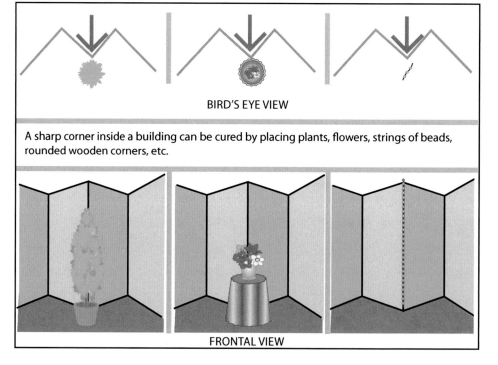

BIRD'S EYE VIEW

A sharp corner inside a building can be cured by placing plants, flowers, strings of beads, rounded wooden corners, etc.

FRONTAL VIEW

3.2.7 BEAMS

Even though your conscious self understands that a ceiling beam is a structural piece that helps keep your house in place and that it is not going to fall, the unconscious mind feels uncomfortable when sitting or sleeping beneath them. Beams can also make you feel oppressed. "Lift" them by using lighter colors, lights, and soft ornaments, like silk flowers, bamboo flutes, or cloth. When placing chairs and beds, avoid having your body symbolically "split" by exposed beams.

3.2.8 OUTDOOR "SHARS"

Sometimes, the roof of another building or the sharp angle of another building can send "shars" to a particular building if that roof or angle points to the latter's façade (or main wall of the building, the one that contains the front door).

Hang a bright object, usually an eight sided mirror (or ba-gua mirror) on the receiving end of the "poison arrow" (where the arrow is pointing at) to deflect the negative energy. The ba-gua mirror is said to disperse the energy in the eight directions, but nevertheless if you are forced to use one, I recommend you say a prayer for those who inhabit the "source" of the poison arrow, so that no harm may come to them.

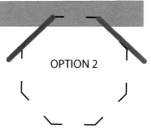

OPTION 1

OPTION 2

Two bamboo flutes hung alongside an exposed beam forming an angle that suggests an octagon, can be used to cure the cutting and oppressive chi produced by the beams.

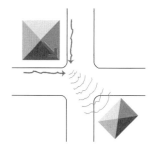

A small (no bigger than 6") octagonal mirror can be placed above a door to deflect the energy from a poison arrow.

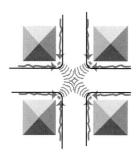

Intersecting shars account for chaotic energy at four way crossroads.

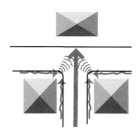

The building at the end of a "T" intersection is in an inauspicious location.

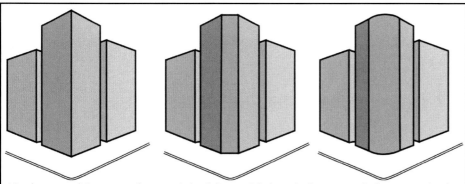

Modern architecture has favored sharp angles for corner buildings. These send chaotic chi towards the intersection and the buildings placed on the opposite corner.

A building with beveled or rounded corners looks more attractive and takes advantage of the full visibility allowed by the corner. Four way intersections where all buildings have considered this are some of the most popular and successful business sites.

NEVER use a ba-gua mirror inside of a building, as you would be duplicating and redirecting the negative energy inside of your own space.

3.2.9 FOUR WAY CROSSROADS AND "T" INTERSECTIONS

Wherever roads intersect, there is a greater chance of accidents than in the middle of one. Even when there are no accidents, close calls will cause people to fret and even curse at each other. The screeching of brakes and the noise of horns blowing are also frequent. All of these cause strained and disturbing chi.

If your home is located at a corner lot, especially if it is by a busy intersection, insulate your lot from the road by using solid fencing, trees and hedges. You can also hang wind chimes in between the building and the intersection, or place a symbol of protection related to your personal faith.

Buildings located at "T" intersections are especially vulnerable because cars seem to be heading directly towards them and , however improbable, the physical possibility exists of a vehicle crashing into the property. In this case too you can use vegetation and fencing to create a real or virtual barrier between the lot and the road, and you can use symbols of protection that face the road. If possible, avoid having the entry to the property in direct alignment with that of the road. The fence's gate should not be directly across from the entrance to the building either. If you can arrange to have a side entrance, that will help too.

3.3 PREVENT STAGNATION AND DRAINS

3.3.1 ALWAYS DO SOMETHING WITH INSIDE CORNERS

Chi tends to get stagnated in the inside of corners

Place one of the following in every corner:

- a plant, preferably live (but silk will work too)
- a light source
- a bright object or mobile (except wind chime)
- corner furniture

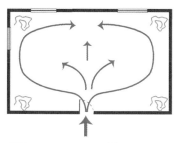

Chi gets stagnated in corners.

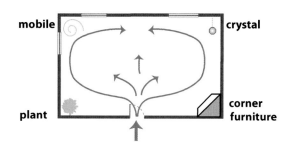

mobile · crystal · plant · corner furniture

Cure the corners of every room.

There are ways to counteract the negativity contained in bathrooms:

Problem #1. Bathrooms contain "dead" energy in that they are the place where we clean ourselves, releasing dead skin cells and hair, and it is also where we dispose of bodily wastes.

Advice. Keep the bathroom very clean and the door to the bathroom closed. Avoid using soft materials that absorb energy, like rugs, mats and curtains, but if you do have them, wash them often.

Problem #2. In bathrooms there are toilets and drains that pull down chi energy.

Advice. Keep drains covered and the toilet lid down.

Problem #3. We find sources of impending danger in bathrooms, that is, items that are potentially dangerous, like razors and strong cleaning agents.

Advice. Keep dangerous items properly put away in cabinets and drawers.

Problem #4. There is an excess of the water element.

Advice. Favor earthy colors like yellow and beige and things made of ceramic or other materials that come from earth. You can also add green plants or images of forests and gardens. The earth and wood (or tree) element absorb water.

3.3.2 LET CHI CIRCULATE

- Let doors open fully and with no obstructions

- Leave pathways, hallways, lobbies and staircases free of any objects that might hinder circulation

- Put nothing under beds, sofas, chairs and tables

- Leave some free room in cabinets and drawers, so that you can find things easily

- Make the bed every day and change the sheets and pillowcases regularly.

- Open curtains, blinds, windows and doors whenever possible to let the sunshine in and to allow air flow.

- Embrace change, **anticipating it** rather than trying to catch up with it.

3.3.3 BATHROOMS

Because of their function, and no matter how clean you keep them, bathrooms contain particles of human waste in the form of hair, dead cells and bodily fluids. Additionally, these rooms host a number of objects that are potentially dangerous (especially in the hands of children) like razors, prescription drugs and strong cleaning agents. They are also the source of unpleasant odors. Bathroom vents are designed to work in a closed room. Therefore, **keep bathroom doors closed**. Hang a full-length mirror on the **outside**, (not the inside) of bathroom doors to bring in the positive energy of the rest of the building.

Accessorize with warm colors and keep all bathrooms well ventilated and place in them some source of good scents.

33

3.3.4 HOLES & DRAINS

This refers to the toilet & drains. Presumably, we have all experienced—directly or indirectly—the loss of some small object that fell in the toilet, sink or floor drains. When any of these orifices is uncovered, fears of losing things are triggered in our minds. These fears can "drain" our energy as well.

That is why we say things like: " the business went down the toilet," or "the money went down the drain." So, keep drains covered when not in use, and keep the toilet lid down.

3.4 UNUSUAL ARCHITECTURAL FEATURES

3.4.1 IRREGULAR SHAPES

(Of rooms, buildings, or properties)

In Feng Shui we say that irregular or strange shapes make chi get confused or behave in erratic ways.

To correct irregular angles (less or more than 90°) follow these criteria:

Closed (acute) angles: place a plant or a round table with a flower arrangement on top.

Wide (obtuse) angles: place light fixtures (lamp, light post, spotlight, etc.)

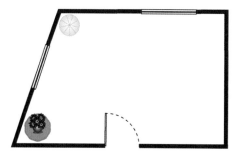 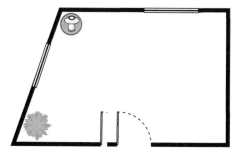

3.4.2 SLANTED WALLS

Modern architects experimented defying the conventional shapes of buildings, especially those devoted to business. Among other things, they played with the slant of walls, both horizontal (producing the irregular shapes we saw above) and vertical (producing walls that do not stand upright). These may have looked interesting from an aesthetic point of view –they are certainly different– but the inhabitants of such places experience strong feelings of instability and oppression. Some have even acquired a tilt in their necks, from unconscious attempts to keep parallel to the walls. Slanted walls are also common in attics.

Even on very steep hills and mountains, healthy trees grow vertical, not slanted. If you are dealing with walls that are slanted from the vertical, emphasize the up-down direction by hanging elements from the slanted wall, which due to gravity will symbolically fix the slant, as shown in the figure:

People will hit their heads against a slanted wall at one time or another...

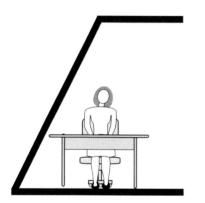

Prisms, bead-strings, ribbons, tassels will hang vertically from the slanted wall and help relieve the uneasiness related to walls that "lean over"

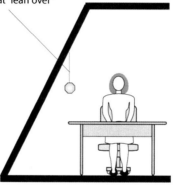

Separate the desk a couple of feet from the wall, if you cannot rotate it as shown in the two bottom figures on the side bar.

... unless you place some kind of furniture, file cabinets, tables, desks along side the wall.

3.5 TOO MANY WINDOWS

When there are too many windows in a building, the chi may leave at a faster pace than it comes in, especially at night. This situation is worsened by windows with no curtains or other treatments, as large windows become large black holes when it is dark outside.

The best solution is to play with adequate window treatments that will reveal some views while hiding others. The simple act of installing valances will help the chi remain, but blinds and curtains will be more effective. However, mini-blinds are not Feng Shui correct as they send cutting energy into the room.

You can also hang stained glass artwork, mobiles (except wind chimes) and plants on the inside of the window. A faceted crystal sphere of about 50 mm diameter hanging from the ceiling in the middle of the room may be of additional help.

To have the desk facing the slanted wall is preferable than to place it sideways like in the previous sample (bottom of the page to the center)...

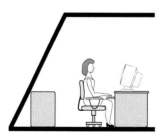

... but facing away from the wall is even better.

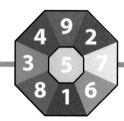

Feng Shui Your Own Home: Key #2

Please answer the questions and follow the instruction in the corresponding sections of the book in the order they are presented. After you complete each task, come back to this key and go to the next question.

1. Are all your clocks showing the right time? Are all your calendars showing the right date?
- ☐ Yes   Go to the next question
- ☐ No   Go to item #4.1

2. Do you have the outside of your home reflect the current season?
- ☐ Yes   Go to the next question
- ☐ No   Go to item #4.2

3. Go to item # 4.3 to learn about the functions of your home's entrance and how you can make it more welcoming.

4. Are you building a home or planning to change the windows?
- ☐ Yes   Go to item # 4.4.1
- ☐ No   Go to the next question

5. Are you satisfied with the curtains or other window treatments in your home?
- ☐ Yes   Go to item # 4.4.2
- ☐ No   Go to the next question

6. Are you planning to re-decorate any rooms in your home and need to decide what style to go with?

☐ Yes   Go to items # 4.4.3 and #8.10
☐ No   Go to the next question

7. Do you want to learn how to combine colors in your home?

☐ Yes   Go to item # 5.1
☐ No   Go to the next question

8. Are you trying to decide what color to paint a particular room in your home?

☐ Yes   Go to item # 5.2
☐ No   Go to the next question

9. Would you like to learn what proportions you should use to put one color next to the other?

☐ Yes   Go to item #5.3
☐ No   Go to the next question

10. Do you need to correct a color clash in your home?

☐ Yes   Go to item # 5.4
☐ No   Go to the next question

11. Are you confronted with a crazy color situation you need to fix?

☐ Yes   Go to item # 5.5
☐ No   Go to the next question

12. Learn how you can use patterns, shapes and materials to harmonize an area.

Go to item # 5.6

13. Is the sink in your kitchen opposite the stove? Or is the stove less than 3 feet from the stove?

☐ Yes   Go to item # 5.7
☐ No   Go to the next question

14. Go to item #6.1 to learn what objects to place at a high, medium or low height.

15. Are you planning to move?
☐ Yes   Go to item # 6.2 to learn what neighborhoods to avoid.
            Go to item #6.6.1 to learn how to choose a safe
            neighborhood.
☐ No   Go to the next question

16. Is the lot in which your home was built flat?
☐ Yes   Go to the next question
☐ No   Go to item #6.3

17. Go to item #6.4 to learn how water relates to money in Feng Shui and what are positive ways to use water and water images.

18. Are you concerned with the quality of your tap water?
☐ Yes   Go to item #6.5
☐ No   Go to the next question

19. Do you live in an area of great natural beauty that you can see through your windows?
☐ Yes   Go to the next question
☐ No   Go to item #6.6.2 to learn how to choose artwork that will
            make you feel like you are surrounded by natural beauty.

20 . Are you happy with your choice of ornaments?
☐ Yes   Go to the next question
☐ No   Go to item 6.6.3

21. Do you know which objects from nature are Feng Shui correct and which are not?
☐ Yes   Go to the next question.
☐ No   Go to item #6.6.4

22. Do you know which plants and flower arrangements are Feng Shui correct and which are not?

☐ Yes   **Go to the next question.**
☐ No   **Go to item #6.6.5 and #6.6.6**

23. Do you have pets?

☐ Yes   **Go to item #6.6.7**
☐ No   **Go to the next question**

24. Do you know which objects from the sea are Feng Shui correct and which are not?

☐ Yes   **Go to the next question.**
☐ No   **Go to item #6.6.8**

25. Do you have a bug problem?

☐ Yes   **Go to item #6.6.8**
☐ No   **Go to the next question**

26. Go to items #6.7 and 6.8 to learn about the role of lights and sound in Feng Shui.

27. Answer these questions about photographs:

Do you display photos anywhere in your home that represent your dreams and aspirations in life?   ☐ Yes   ☐ No

Do you have pictures of you and your partner (if applicable) that show you both happy, handsome and loving?   ☐ Yes   ☐ No

Do you display photos of your nuclear family in a prominent place?
☐ Yes   ☐ No

Do you know where to place photos of the extended family and friends?
☐ Yes   ☐ No

Do you display photos of your parents, no matter what your relationship with them is like? ☐ Yes ☐ No

Do you have self worth issues? ☐ Yes ☐ No

Go to item #6.9.1 to learn the basic Feng Shui guidelines for displaying photographs.

27. Answer these questions about mirrors:

Are there any beveled mirrors in your home? ☐ Yes ☐ No

Do you have any mirror tiles or mirrored double doors?
☐ Yes ☐ No

Do the mirrors in your bathroom meet at the corner?
☐ Yes ☐ No

Do you keep any convex or concave mirrors? ☐ Yes ☐ No

Do you have any mirrors with exposed edges (no frames)?
☐ Yes ☐ No

Go to item #6.10 to learn the basic Feng Shui guidelines for mirrors.

When you are done with this section you can move on to Key #3 on page 86.

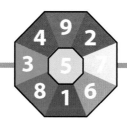

Feng Shui Your Own Home

Step

Work With Nature

At any time we can choose whether to go with nature or against it.

We tend to do a lot better when we tune in to the rhythms, movements and energies of nature.

STEP FOUR: WORK WITH NATURE

There is a basic rhythm in all of Creation that is expressed in the movement of our planet as well as in our breathing. The seasons of the year, the hours in a day, the phases of the moon, all revolve around this basic pattern. When we live by that rhythm we tend to do better

This basic rhythm has four energetic movements:

- **Rising** energy: spring / dawn and morning / crescent moon / inhaling / East

- **Radiating** energy: summer / Midday / full moon / full lung expansion / South (Northern Hemisphere) or North (Southern Hemisphere)

- **Descending** energy: fall / afternoon and sunset / waning moon/ exhaling / West

- **Halting** energy: winter / 12 midnight / new moon / emptying of the lungs in preparation for the next breathing cycle / North (Northern Hemisphere) or South (Southern Hemisphere)

All clocks and calendars should show the right time and the right date.

4.1 TIME AND TIMING - CALENDARS AND CLOCKS

In order for us to be able to take advantage of opportunities we need to be at the right place at the right time, and for us to do this it is necessary that we become aware of the current time.

To show the Universe you are lined up with the current energies of time and timing, all clocks must be in good working condition and show the right time and all calendars must show the right day, week or month.

Clocks and calendars that do not show the current date and time create an element of distrust within the home. For example, if you are getting ready to go and need to check the time, your mind directs you to the nearest clock. When you look up (or down) at it, if the clock has recently stopped you are not aware that it is showing an incorrect time, you might be early or late to wherever you need to go. However if the clock has stopped working for a while, almost as soon as you see it, you will remember that you cannot go by what it says (you cannot trust it). Much peace of mind can be added to a home by making sure that all clocks, watches and calendars are set to reflect true dates and times.

4.2 A SEASONAL ENTRANCE

Dates and times are artificially created ways to track the passing of time, but they don't necessarily reflect what is going on in nature at any given time. For example, Christmas weather in the United States is very different from Christmas weather in Australia.

Place some reminder of the current season right outside the front door. Whenever possible include seasonal flowers.

You can also place a reminder of the current holiday right outside your front door or somewhere in the front yard.

4.3 A BUFFER FOR OUTSIDE ENERGIES

The energy outside your home is very different from the energy inside your home. The outside world is related to challenges. Inside the home is the space where you get renewed, where your batteries are re-charged.

Outside of the home are the struggles for life — traffic jams, noise, stressful jobs, deadlines, catering to clients, dealing with co-workers — you name it. The hectic activities of life in the city charge our auras or energy fields with less than love frequencies.

Make the entrance to your home into a buffer or filter that allows some kind of ceremony, ritual or even just plain routine, for you to unwind from the stresses of the external world.

Essential to this buffer are two welcome mats or a welcome mat and a rug. There should be a welcome mat outside your home that is proportional to the size of your front door. The welcome mat represents cleaning your soul from the energies of the outer world just as you clean the mud, grass, dust, etc. from your shoes.

As you enter the home you need to step on an additional filter for impurities and dirt gathered on the outside but also a soft surface on

You don't have to go overboard, (though you can) but simply adding one or two objects that are a reminder of the season by the front door will help you connect to the rhythms of nature.

A welcome mat is essential. It doesn't have to have the word "welcome" printed on it, but if it does then you should be able to read the words in the right direction as you are coming in from the outside. A rug in the foyer symbolizes the softer side of life.

Hinged windows are excellent choices for rooms on the ground floor. In areas where mosquitoes and other bugs are a problem during the hot weather, this type of window becomes inconvenient because of the need for screens.

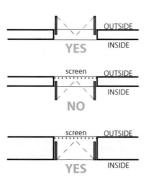

You can still have a hinged window and keep the screens if the walls are very thick, such as adobe walls or insulated concrete walls that would allow you to open the window and not have the window pane in the way.

which to step making that transition between the rougher material of the welcome mat to the softer more elegant nature of the welcome rug inside the home is very symbolic and positive. If you can, change your welcome mat seasonally.

If possible, repeat this concept of "welcome mat/inside rug" in all the doors in your home that lead to the outside.

If you can, place a flower arrangement in your foyer that reminds you of the season or your current holiday. You can extrapolate this idea by placing a seasonal or holiday-related low center piece or table cloth on the dining table.

4.4 WINDOWS AND THE CONNECTION TO THE OUTSIDE WORLD

Windows are the main regulators of the relationship between the home and the areas outside of the home.

Windows and window treatments allow us to choose whether to let light in or not and whether to let fresh air in or not. How we use this power of choice depends on our personal preferences, the outside weather and other conditions, such as the location of the home. In order to have this choice, however, **it is paramount that every single room in your home have a window you can easily access and open.**

4.4.1 TYPES OF WINDOWS -THINGS YOU NEED TO KNOW WHEN CHOOSING WINDOWS

4.4.1.1 HINGED WINDOWS: BEST ON THE GROUND FLOOR

When Feng Shui came to be window panes were mounted on wooden frames and hinged to the sides much like double doors. It was a time when homes were not very high and windows afforded a direct connection with the outside. This is not only particular of classical Chinese architecture but also of many other cultures, like southern European and Middle Eastern cultures.

Hinged windows are easy to reach and open, so they tend to be opened more. They also open completely, offering a greater connection with the outside than you would get from other types of windows.

From the second floor on though, this same ease of opening can become a problem, since it makes it easier to drop things down the window and it increases the potential of someone falling out the window at a height where this could be fatal.

Crank windows and other types of casement windows are usually considered as "good Feng Shui."

4.4.1.2 SLIDING TO THE SIDES YES, UP AND DOWN NO!

Windows that slide from one side to another (horizontally) are an excellent Feng Shui choice at any height.

However double hung sash windows or single hung sash windows are not recommended, because of two reasons: they are hard to reach and open, usually requiring strength, and the up and down movement resembles a guillotine.

4.4.1.3 OPENING ABOVE BETTER THAN BELOW

Open windows must provide a connection with the outside at face level or higher to be effective.

Double hung sash windows thus, though not Feng Shui correct, are still better than single hung sash windows, which only allow a relationship with the outdoors at belly level or below (for adults).

4.4.1.4 DON'T KICK MY WINDOW!

Feng Shui recommends not having windows that go all the way to the floor. Window sills should be at least as high as knee level. Even though your window may be bullet proof, the unconscious mind still perceives glass that is too close to the floor as a cause for potential accidents.

4.4.2 CURTAINS AND WINDOW TREATMENTS

Windows can expose us to or shield us from the outside world.

In many American homes I see a tendency to not have curtains or other kinds of window treatments when the house is located in rural areas with beautiful views, or at the back of homes urban areas where there is a fenced in back yard and beautiful grounds. Although during the day plenty of positive chi comes in through the windows, night time is a different story. There are two reasons why you shouldn't leave windows uncovered at night: the first one is that when the lights are on, your family life is put on a window case, where people from the

Single hung sash windows are not Feng Shui correct. They resemble a guillotine, age poorly, and are a potential danger to little fingers or animal tails when closing.

Window openings need to connect us to the energies of heaven, to hope and insight. Windows that open on top also offer better ventilation, as smells, just like heat and smoke tend to go up.

This window presents two Feng Shui problems: first it is a single-hung window which only opens at the bottom, second the awning shutter opens from the bottom.

Windows with no curtains or other kinds of window treatments may look OK during the day, but at night they become a black hole that drains the energy of the home.

outside could observe you and this not only makes the unconscious mind uncomfortable but it also poses a very real security issue. The second reason is that the absence of light turns the window into a black square or rectangle which creates a yin (dark, cold, humid, weak) imbalance in the home, as well as adding too much of the water element, which is related to the color black (this relationship will be discussed more in depth in the next chapter.)

Mini blinds are not Feng Shui friendly. They provide a fragmented view of the world and the relative sharpness of every single stripe sends cutting energy into the room.

Accordion blinds are better choices, but remember, it is better to get the kind that open from the top and allow you a view of the sky than the kind that open from the bottom.

Good Feng Shui windows and window treatment combinations.

4.4.3 THE RHYTHMS OF NATURE AND THE ROOMS IN THE HOME

Let's see how the four energies in the basic rhythm of the planet are expressed in the seasons:

- **Spring** is the season for awakening, for rapid growth and reproduction. New hopes arise as we see life being restored from apparent death. There seem to be so many possibilities, so much potential. The earth gets filled with flowers an their aromas, baby animals running about, flocks of birds flying overhead... and people working on the land, taking care of their farms or gardens or pots, planting seeds, investing for the future.

  Spring functions with a bursting, **rising** energy. This is the kind of energy that benefits both the dining area and the kitchen.

- When **Summer** arrives we are all drawn to the outdoors. The days are longer. Having everything under the sun makes all things in creation more visible. It is harder to hide anything, even our bodies, since we usually cover them less in the summer. During the day we look for shady places and like to be near the coolness of water, and in the evening life in the streets is more active during this season – we go to outdoor cafes and restaurants, fairs, music festivals, bonfires, etc.

  Summer works with an energy of **radiation**. Going from the inside out, like the rays of the sun. This is the kind of energy that benefits the Family Room and the Master Bedroom.

- In the **Fall**, we reap what we have sowed. It is a time for rewards or regrets. An abundant harvest awakens in us strong feelings of gratitude towards our Creator and towards nature. We get much more than what we invested.

  The falling of the leaves and the fading of the colors remind us that we need to prepare ourselves for the cold and stillness of the winter, and use what we have wisely. In short, two different kind of feelings coexist: one, rejoicing in the fruits of the earth and celebrating our blessings; and the other one, concern for the future.

  The energy of Fall is one of **descent**, of calming down, settling. This kind of energy benefits Children's Bedrooms, Arts and Crafts rooms and Hobby Rooms, as well as the Living Room and Altars.

- In **Winter** most activities in nature have ceased, they remain latent. Animals migrate or hide in their lairs, some even hibernate in wait for better weather that will make life easier in the outside. But there is an undercurrent of energy, which is being restored and contained, getting ready for new beginnings.

  People stay home more, they read, they study, reflect, go inside, analyze, evaluate the past year. This is also a good time for fixing things inside the house, repairing and buying tools for the upcoming spring. It is cold, and we yearn for sunnier days.

  The winter energy is one of **halting**, of apparent calm, but hidden preparation and planning. This kind of energy benefits the foyer, hallways and staircases, as well as Offices, Studies and Libraries.

4.4.3.1 THE ENERGIES OF EVERY ROOM

If you want to take this step farther, you can give each room the general mood suggested by the corresponding season, time of the day, and phase of the moon.

ROOM	SEASON	TIME OF DAY	PHASE OF THE MOON
Entries and circulation areas	EARLY WINTER	MIDNIGHT	NEW MOON
Master Bedroom	LATE SUMMER	AFTERNOON	FULL MOON
Dining Room	EARLY SPRING	DAWN	CRESCENT MOON
Kitchen	LATE SPRING	MORNING	CRESCENT MOON
Living Room, Sanctuary, Altar	LATE FALL	EVENING	WANING MOON
Children's Bedrooms, Art Studio	EARLY FALL	SUNSET	WANING MOON
Home Office or Study	LATE WINTER	NIGHT	NEW MOON
Family Room	EARLY SUMMER	NOON	FULL MOON

For example, if you are thinking of decorating a dining room, imagine you were taking a walk shortly after sunrise in the early spring. What would the air feel like? What colors would you see? What would you hear? Think about the general mood you will perceive — this is the kind of feeling that you would want to reproduce for your dining area.

If you wanted to decorate a master bedroom on the other hand, you would think of an afternoon in the late summer. The mood of the late summer includes heat and dryness and rich colors, so you would want to choose rich, warm colors, and you would want to avoid cool colors and images of water.

For any room, use your imagination to make a mental picture of what the corresponding season feels like at the particular time of the day that goes with it and make your decisions for the general feel of the room based on this information.

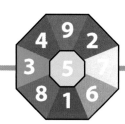

Feng Shui Your Own Home

Step

5

Harmonize Colors

Color has deep physical and psychological effects in people.

In Feng Shui, five different families of colors interact with each other in a complex system of checks and balances, which has a relationship with feelings, moods, and even with systems and organs in our bodies.

Each element is related to a family of colors:

The deep waters are dark. Black, navy blue, eggplant color, dark hard woods... any color that at a distance might be perceived as black form a part of the water element.

The wood element represents live plants, where the predominant color is the color of foliage. All shades of green, teal, aqua, turquoise and light blues are part of the wood element.

The fire element is present in all red shades, bright oranges and lemon yellow, burgundy and purples (with a greater proportion of red than blue).

STEP FIVE: HARMONIZE COLORS

While it is true that color is largely a matter of taste, Feng Shui color theory has parallels with the way Traditional Chinese Medicine addresses health, and each family of colors has a resonance with two organs and one system in our bodies.

In Feng Shui color decisions are made based on Five Elements Theory.

The five elements are: **Water, Wood, Fire, Earth, and Metal.**

We feel in harmony with nature when objects representative of each element are present in a room. Some representation of each of the five elements must always be present in order to have a harmonious space, but the proportions vary according to the different rooms and needs.

Each of the five elements is related to a family of colors:

ELEMENT	FAMILY OF COLORS
Water	Black, navy blue and any other deep dark colors WE CALL THIS THE **DEEP DARK FAMILY** OF COLORS
Wood	All shades of green, sky blue, baby blue and teal WE CALL THIS THE **TREE TONES FAMILY** OF COLORS (we mean the foliage, not the trunk)
Fire	All shades of red, bright oranges and lemon yellow WE CALL THIS THE **FIERY RED TONES FAMILY** OF COLORS
Earth	Yellow, brown, mustard, terracota and other earth tones WE CALL THIS THE **EARTH TONES FAMILY** OF COLORS
Metal	White, gray, mauve and metallic colors WE CALL THIS THE **WHITE AND SILVER TONES** FAMILY OF COLORS

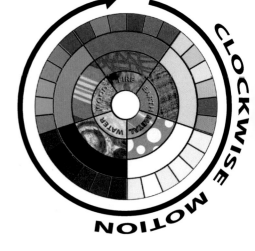

Each of these families of colors gets along with two other families (the ones that are placed next to it in the circle), and clashes with two of the families (the ones that are not touching in the circle).

Usually you want to work with two families of colors that are touching each other as the dominant colors in a room. When you do this, the one located to the left, if you consider a clockwise motion, should be used in a larger proportion than the one at its right. Then the other three colors can be used in a much lesser proportion than the first two.

Five elements theory is one of the hardest parts of Feng Shui to understand and use properly, so rather than giving you a lot of theory here, I am going to show you visually how families of colors are addressed in Feng Shui.

5.1 COLOR HARMONIES IN THE HOME: A PROVEN FORMULA

You can have a harmonious home using many different colors and combinations. People with an "eye for color" are able to choose the right hues and shades to create comfortable and creative spaces.

However, for most people, who haven't had specific training when it comes to colors it is safer to stick with proven color combinations. What this means essentially is to work with a base of earth tones and then add accents to that or to stick with earth tones on all painted walls and bigger pieces of furniture, while experimenting with color accents in artwork and accessories.

Most interior designs of homes emphasize earth tones, followed by tree tones (greens and light blues) and white/silver tones. Dark tones and fiery red tones are usually used only as accents.

All the colors of soil, dirt and sand, like brown, yellow and beige, and all the skin colors form part of the earth element.

White, gray, mauve and all pastel colors are part of the metal element, as well as all shiny and metallic colors, like gold, silver and copper.

WATER **feeds** WOOD

WOOD **feeds** FIRE

FIRE **produces** EARTH

EARTH **yields** METAL

METAL **carries** WATER

Next I will show you an example of how to work with color in a living or family room where the dominant family of colors is earth.

Imagine that you have rented a place that has light hardwood floors and yellow ocher walls.

The predominant family of colors is the earth tones family.

I am using for this example a neutral ceiling color (in homes the ceiling is usually painted white or off-white to add light by reflecting window and lamp light, and is not included in the analysis of colors). If we were talking about businesses, however, we would consider the ceiling colors.

If you look at the circle in the previous page you will see that in the clockwise direction the color family that follows Earth is the white/silver family. So an off-white couch and chair have been added, as well as white curtains and a painting in mainly pastel tones (pastel tones are part of the white/silver family because they are mostly white).

In this drawing you see how the deep dark tones have been added by using dark wooden furniture.

While most woods would be part of the earth tones, it is not so with very dark woods, whatever the hue. Any color that is dark enough that it might look black in the distance or in photograph is part of the deep dark tones family.

Next in line is the Tree family of colors which includes all shades of green and some light blues. A green rug and a green plant have been placed. (There are also some blues and greens in the painting).

Finally, in the last graphic, we add the remaining family of colors, Fiery Reds, as a small accent. Red goes a long way, so it only takes a little bit to add the energy of fire contained in this family.

Of course the graphics in this example show only the very basic furniture and accessories you might have in a living or family room, but they can give you an idea of how to work with families of colors, adding them in a particular order and making sure to reduce the proportions of each family of colors you add as you go along.

In these two pages I have shown you the most common color harmonies used in the interior design of homes, which follows the proportions in the graphic below:

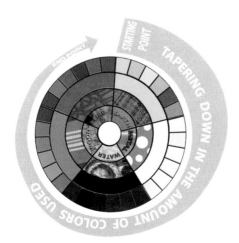

Now I will show you some examples of the same living or family room layout but starting out with different base colors.

On the left we see a living or family room that has the white/silver tones family of colors in the floor and walls.

The color family to the right of this one

is the deep dark tones family, so a black entertainment center, tables and accessories have been used, followed by the tree family of colors in the couch and chairs, curtains and a green plant. The fire family comes in with a crimson red carpet and basket, and finally the earth tones are represented by a simple ornament placed on the table.

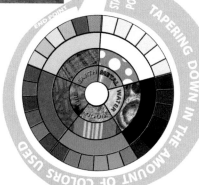

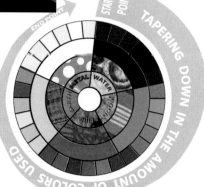

Imagine that you have moved into a place with a very dark colored carpet, but where you are allowed to paint the walls. The family of colors that follows

the deep dark tones is the Tree family, so a sage green has been used for the walls. The fire tones come in with red-wood furniture and door and curtains to match, as well as some apples on the table. The couch and chairs are in earth tones, and finally there is a white lamp and an off-white rug to bring in the last family of colors as an accent.

Below we have a classic striped wall paper in green and light blue tones and a teal carpet, all part of the tree tones family of colors. The color family that follows is the fire tones one, but you have to be careful when combining greens and reds, lest you end up with a Christmas look. A safe way to add the fire

tones is to use red woods, which you can see in some of the furniture, the door and the trimming. A painting with red flowers has also been used. The couch and chairs are in earth tones, as well as the cream colored rug. Off-white curtains and lamps bring in the white/silver tones and there is only one accent in a deep dark tone.

Finally, a space that starts off with floors in the fire tones. The walls have been painted with an earth tones color, but a painting with

a lot of reds has been added because the wall surface is greater than the floor surface and we have to be careful that the earth tones do not overpower the fire tones. Plenty of white/silver tones are present in the furniture, curtains and rug, some deep dark tones in the rest of the furniture and tree tones are expressed only minimally.

5.2 COLORS FOR DIFFERENT ROOMS

The chart in this page shows you what are the dominant colors recommended in Feng Shui for each of the rooms in the home. Take a look at this chart and compare it to the actual colors you have in the corresponding rooms in your home.

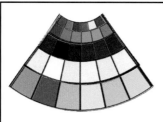

FIRE
WOOD
WATER
METAL
EARTH

Earth dominant color combinations work well for the master bedroom.

WOOD
WATER
METAL
EARTH
FIRE

Fire dominant color combinations work well for the family room.

WATER
METAL
EARTH
FIRE
WOOD

Wood dominant color combinations work well for the dining room and kitchen.

METAL
EARTH
FIRE
WOOD
WATER

Water dominant color combinations are not recommended for homes. though they can be used in some businesses.

EARTH
FIRE
WOOD
WATER
METAL

Metal dominant color combinations work well for formal living rooms and children's rooms.

5.3 COLOR FAMILIES THAT GET ALONG: COLOR PROPORTIONS

Families of colors that are next to each other in the circle are better combined if the one on the left, when reading the chart clockwise, is in greater proportion than the one on the right. The family of colors on the left is considered the "mother" of the family of colors on the right, and you always want to make sure that the "mother" is bigger than the "child."

You may want to get a piece of white paper and cover up one side of this page at a time and note your reactions to each.

Every single element is considered the "mother" of the element that follows it clockwise (on the elements wheel), and this applies to the colors of the elements too:

These color combinations ("child" bigger than the mother") slow down the energy.

These color combinations ("mother" larger than the "child") energize a space.

WATER IS THE MOTHER OF WOOD

Deep dark tones are the mother of the tree tones

WOOD IS THE MOTHER OF FIRE

Tree tones are the mother of the fiery red tones

FIRE IS THE MOTHER OF EARTH

Fiery red tones are the mother of earth tones

EARTH IS THE MOTHER OF METAL

Earth tones are the mother of the white/gray/pastel tones

METAL IS THE MOTHER OF WATER

White/silver tones are the mother of the deep dark tones

5.4 CORRECTING COLOR CONFLICTS AND CLASHES

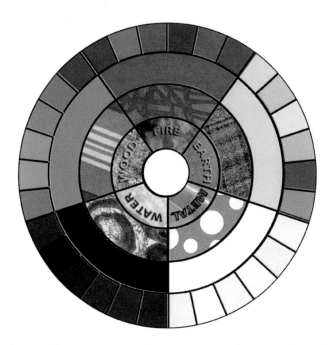

When you have **close to equal amounts** of two color families that compete with each other (colors that are not next to each other) you can reconcile the clash by adding the color of the element that is in between them in the circle.

The Dark Deep Tones clash with the Fire Tones, but only when the Tree Tones are missing.

Tree Tones clash with Earth Tones, but only when the Fire Tones are missing.

Fire Tones clash with the White/Silver Tones, but only when the Earth Tones are missing.

Earth Tones clash with the Deep Dark Tones, but only when the White, Off-white and Gray are missing.

The White/Silver Tones clash with the Tree tones, but only when the Deep Dark Tones are missing.

So the solution to color clashes, when two families of colors have been used in close to equal proportions, is to add the family of colors that **is between** them in the circle. Take a look at the particular cases in the next two pages.

When green and white are used in large areas and equal proportions there is a color clash.

You can resolve this conflict by adding colors in the Deep Dark Tones family.

When red and black (or another very dark color like navy blue) are used in large areas and equal proportions there is a color clash.

You can resolve this conflict by adding greens and light blues from the Tree Tones family of colors.

When green and orange, yellow or brown are used in large areas and equal proportions there is a color clash.

You can resolve this conflict by adding colors from the Fire Tones family.

When red and white are used in large areas and equal proportions there is a color clash.

You can resolve this conflict by adding colors in the Earth Tones family.

When yellow/orange and black are used in large areas and equal proportions there is a color clash.

You can resolve this conflict by adding colors in the White/Silver Tones family.

The elements in the human body

The five elements that are used to harmonize colors in Feng Shui also have an expression in the human body, each of them corresponds to two organs, a system and an extension

 The water element is related to the kidneys and bladder, the bones, the ear and the hair on the scalp.

 The wood element is related to the bladder and gallbladder, the muscles, the eyes, and the nails.

 The fire element is related to the heart and small intestine, and the veins and arteries, and complexion color (cheeks).

 The earth element is related to the stomach and spleen, body fat, connective tissues, and the lips.

 The metal element is related to the lungs and large intestine, the skin and bodily hair.

5.5 CRAZY COLOR SITUATIONS AND HOW TO CORRECT THEM

Sometimes it happens that for whatever reason someone has decorated a room using only one family of colors. This creates an uneasy feeling in most people. Even some dramatic interior that you may like on first impression, if it was designed with one family of colors only, becomes hard to live with day in and day out.

When faced with this kind of situation, first identify the family of colors that has been used, then count two families of colors on the circle, but this time counterclockwise. The second family is the one that destroys the energy of the one you are dealing with.

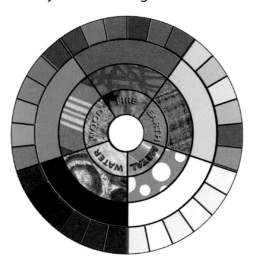

For example, if you have a room that has been done all in Earth Tones and feels dry and uninteresting, you count backwards (counterclockwise) two times and arrive at the Tree Tones family. This means that by adding a touch of greens or light blues you can liven up the drab environment created by too many yellows and browns.

Keep in mind that any changes you make need not only be effective from the Feng Shui point of view, but should also be appealing to your own taste and sense of aesthetics.

In the next page you will see some examples of some crazy color situations you might encounter and how to do quick fixes.

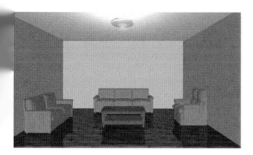

5.5.1 CRAZY COLOR SITUATION 1: TOO MUCH YELLOW OR BROWN

Let's imagine that an aunt and uncle are letting you use their cabin for a two week vacation in the mountains. When you get there you find that the floors, walls and ceiling are made of wood, so it is all brown or yellow. Furthermore, the furniture is brown or yellow. This feels too earthy, dry and drab. A quick fix to make the place more comfortable during your stay would be to add some light blue or green accents, especially live green plants. Remember not to add too much green or light blue though, as this would create a clash instead of a fix.

5.5.2 CRAZY COLOR SITUATION 2: TOO MUCH WHITE AND/OR GRAY

Say that a friend has asked you to house sit their home for one month. Your friend has decorated everything in white or light gray and the place gives you the impression of a sterile clinical environment. It feels cold and unwelcoming. The quick fix for this situation is to add some red or reddish accents, like some ornaments or candles, or even a platter of red apples. If you add too much red though, you will create a clash.

5.5.3 CRAZY COLOR SITUATION 3: TOO MUCH BLACK OR DEEP BLUE

When faced with a space that has very dark floors, dark walls and dark furniture, adding some objects in the earth family of colors will relieve the heavy, sad feeling the dark colors can give. In the example above we have added a couple of light wood tables and yellow lamps. If you add too much yellow or brown, you will create a clash.

5.5.4 CRAZY COLOR SITUATION 4: TOO MUCH GREEN OR LIGHT BLUE

Imagine that a great aunt has left you a historic home in her will and that you don't want to make any changes until you have done more research and save the money to do them right. The living room has green carpet, and green wall paper. There is an excess of the Trees family of colors here, accentuated by the vertical stripes which are reminiscent of tree trunks.

The way to temporarily fix this color problem is to add a few white accents. As with all color corrections, adding too much of the correcting color would create a clash instead of a fix.

5.5.4 CRAZY COLOR SITUATION 5: TOO MUCH RED

Say some friends of yours have to do some repairs in their home and a third friend has offered them their finished basement to stay while they wait for their home to be ready. They step into the basement and they think they have been transported to a bad disco club — it's all red. Your friends could make this place easier to live in during their short stay by adding some black accents. Again, if they added too much black they would create a new problem instead of a fix.

5.6 USING PATTERNS, SYMBOLS AND OBJECTS

Just as the five elements are represented in certain colors, they are also expressed in particular patterns. So if you want to include an element in your interior design but don't particularly like the color(s) related to that element you can use the pattern of the element instead:

The **water** element is expressed in wavy patterns as well as in free-form organic shapes, and in glass objects and images of water.

The **wood** element is expressed in vertical stripes and tall rectangles, and in images of trees and forests.

The **fire** element is expressed in triangles and pyramids, as well as star and sun images.

The **earth** element is expressed in checkered patterns and horizontal stripes and in objects made from clay, ceramic or porcelain.

The **metal** element is expressed in polka dots patterns and spheres, and in any objects made out of metal.

Say for example that you see a room is lacking the fire element, but you really don't like red or you think red wouldn't look good in the room. You

Patterns Representative of each of the Five Elements

Water

Wood

Fire

Earth

Metal

can add the fire element by placing artwork with straight geometrical shapes, especially triangles.

By the same token, you could add the water element by including wave patterns, or a single wave line drawn on a wall to separate two colors, one on top and another one at the bottom. A friend of mine added the water element to a healing center by asking the designers to build S-shaped walls to create an undulating path in the hallway.

Another example, if you would like to have more of the wood element to a room, you don't necessarily have to add more green to the walls or furniture in a room, you may do so by adding more plants, tall and thin objects or vertical stripes.

5.7 STOVE AND SINK CONFLICTS

A common five elements problem found in homes, that is not related to colors is the proximity and location of the sink and the stove in the kitchen. This is a conflict of water putting out fire.

5.7.1 STOVE AND SINK ACROSS FROM EACH OTHER

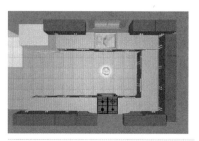

When the stove and sink are across from each other hang a crystal ball from the ceiling in between the two features, as shown in the graphics (the crystal ball is pictured larger than it would be for visibility on the graphic).

5.7.2 LESS THAN 3 ft. OF COUNTER SPACE BETWEEN THE SINK AND THE STOVE

You can hang a crystal, as above, between the two features. You can also place a plant in between the two, especially plants in the bamboo family.

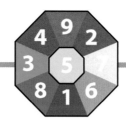

Feng Shui Your Own Home

Step

Using the Right Symbols

People connect to and understand life through symbols and archetypes.

Some symbols are universal for all humans, other symbols are culture-specific, and some symbols are only of family or personal importance.

Using the right symbols ensures that your home gives you the feedback that you are safe, that progress and happiness are possible, and that you are who you wish to be.

STEP SIX: USING THE RIGHT SYMBOLS

Words, symbols and signs are what form **languages**. Languages are used to communicate.

The spaces we inhabit "talk" to us. The careful observation of a room will reveal many things about the person who lives or works in it. The "messages" a space sends us are many times literal. For example "a cluttered house reveals a cluttered mind".

Other people and the universe in general "read" the messages that we and our homes and offices send to the world. There is a Chinese saying, "Everything in your home is talking to you, make sure they have nice things to say."

This section will deal with the most common signs, symbols, and literal translations (from space to life) that are considered in Feng Shui.

6.1 HIGH AND LOW

We tend to elevate the things that we appreciate the most (like awards, certificates, trophies, expensive ornaments), while placing things we don't particularly care for on the floor. We obviously don't care too much for the things we leave on the floor, since they could be kicked or stepped on at any moment. On the other hand, if things are stored too high, beyond the reach of our stretched arms, they become inaccessible to us, unless we get a ladder or stepping stool. This can produce feelings of inadequacy or impotence.

If we get home tired after a day at work and throw the purse – in which we carry our money, checkbooks and debit/credit cards– to the floor, we are sending the message to the universe that we don't care about money or material things. Conventional Western design often assigns hooks or shelves for purses, wallets and keys close to one of the entrance doors, because of the convenience of picking them up on your way out and putting them away as you come in. However this puts your valuables and the access to your home, business, car, too close to an area of the home that can be visited by strangers. Say for example that the doorbell rings and it is the pizza delivery guy. You tell him to wait until you get him a check or cash and walk away from the foyer for a moment. If your keys were hanging from a hook in the foyer this person could easily walk away with your keys.

Place money, purses and wallets in a safe place in your home, hidden or not clearly visible, at about waist or torso height, not too close to the entrance doors. Never leave your bag or wallet on the floor. Hang your keys or place them in a drawer in the same place every day, but, again, not too close to the entrance doors.

Ideally, the floors should be free of anything but furniture and carpets, rugs, or floor mats. High shelves or cabinets should be used to display adornments, certificates or trophies –things we are proud of– and for items we do not use on a regular basis. If I visit a client's home and find that a sports trophy is being used as a doorstop or is on a bottom shelf collecting dust, I will look for other signs of low self esteem in the person who originally won this trophy, or for signs of resentment towards that person from another family member (that has placed the trophy in an appropriate location).

6.2 PAST, PRESENT, AND FUTURE

We always say the future is "ahead" of us and that we should put the past "behind" us. Similarly, in our houses:

The front yard represents the immediate future (what lies ahead). Whatever is across the road from your home affects how you view your future. This is why in Feng Shui we recommend that you do not move into a home that has either of the following across the road:

- Police station
- Fire station
- Church
- Funeral home

The above mentioned places generate anxious thoughts and feelings when we see them. It is very inauspicious to have one of these buildings be the first sight you see as you leave home. You should in general avoid large buildings and any organizations and institutions that would generate a lot of traffic.

House "A" is in a more auspicious position than house "B". When this street floods, house "B" will flood too. If your building is in such a location as "B", place a light post and a spotlight at the bottom of the slope pointing upwards towards the center of the roof.

We tend to "read" buildings from left to right. House "C" gives the impression of a lot *going down"* while house "D" gives the impression of a lot *going up*. House "D" therefore is in a more auspicious position. In either case, you can cure the slope by adding a light post at the lower end.

The house on the left is in a very inauspicious location, being trapped between the hill and the higher building on the right.

Therefore also avoid moving into a home that faces:

- Schools
- Government buildings
- Supermarkets
- Malls

The building itself stands for the present (your life today, in the now). The yard or open space on the left side of the building (as you look at it from the street) is related to how you address the challenges of life, work and effort in general. The yard or open space on the right side of the building is related to how you nourish your life, how you recharge your batteries and how you enjoy yourself.

The back yard represents the immediate past (what we are leaving behind). What is behind your property influences how you relate to your past.

Homes need some form of protection at the back, so having a hill or a forest behind your property is auspicious. A home bigger than yours is also OK. A fence at the back of the property is very helpful, and a must if you lack any of the before mentioned elements behind your property.

A front yard that is too steep poses a problem, as well as one that goes down from the street towards the home. A back yard that slopes away from the home needs to be cured.

6.3 SLOPES

It is much easier to keep your balance when running on a flat surface than it is when walking on terrain that has a slant. The origin of the word "slope" itself means "to slip away". We are talking of "rising" or "falling" ground here.

When confronted with an inclined surface, we instinctively react with concerns of falling down, of losing our ground. Therefore, a flat plot of land is more recommended than an inclined one. A gentle slope in front of the building is OK, but if the slope is on the back yard, it needs to be cured.

These are several ways you can deal with slopes:

- Install a light post or spotlight at the bottom, pointing the light upwards, towards the center or the top of the property.

- Place a tall fence at the bottom of the slope, or plant hedges where covenants forbid fencing.

- Plant a tall tree where the terrain is lower.

- Create a meandering path from top to bottom of the slope so that people walking on it feel safe; either keep the incline low or correct it with a few steps here and there.

- Even out the ground before building when possible (this may not always be an option, for ecological, topographical or aesthetic reasons).

- Create several "terraces" of flat ground, connected between themselves by steps or low-incline ramps. Add hedges balustrades or handrails as necessary for protection.

Look at the graphics on this page and the next one for specific ways to cure slopes. For specific lot problems that you don't find here, please check the Feng Shui your Own Yard manual. (coming out in 2010) or consult a Feng Shui professional.

PROBLEM: the front yard slopes down towards the building.

SOLUTION: Place a horizontal feature in between the street/sidewalk and the house. This will help lessen the feeling of "falling down" into the house that the slope can give. Make sure to also open up a flat area in front of the main door.

PROBLEM: there is a steep slope going down between the street and the house.

SOLUTIONS:

1. Paint the house in bright colors to "lift it up"; 2. Build a retaining wall; 3. Create a flat open area between the house and the beginning of the slope if possible.; 4. Get a large and colorful mail box with flowers and/or garden art.; 5. Get a couple of nice markers to place on each side of the beginning of the driveway from the street or road.

PROBLEM: the front yard is too steep.

SOLUTION: Zig-zag landscaping features and steps going up. The best choice is to have steps in short flights with frequent landings and changing directions. The drawings below show both the side view and the birds eye view of good Feng Shui steps for a very steep yard.

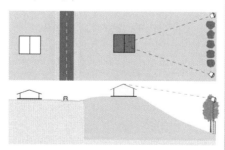

PROBLEM: A Steep Slope Going Down in the Back Yard

SOLUTION: 1. Make sure to have a tall fence at the back of the property or plant a line of tall bushes or trees near the property limit.; 2. Place two light posts at the back corners, preferably spot lights pointing at the top center of the house.

In Feng Shui, water is related to money.

6.4 WATER AND MONEY

Before technology allowed us to easily store and transport water from one place to the other, even long distances, it was basic for survival to build our homes near natural supplies of fresh water, like rivers, streams, lakes, springs, or where underground waters were available through the use of wells. Furthermore, water provides us with fish and seafood, which are great sources of nutrients and minerals for our bodies. It also has allowed us transportation that is smoother, more economical and sometimes even faster than traveling by ground. For thousands of years, it has brought us news and goods from far away places.

- The sound of slowly flowing water calms and gives us confidence, as it reminds us of streams, springs and soft drizzles.

- The sound of rapidly flowing water reminds us of floods, rain storms or hail, which could indicate loss.

Since irrigation is essential for steadier agricultural production (not having to rely on the rain), water is inextricably linked with our idea of prosperity.

Money is also called "currency," a word closely related to "current", which means running or flowing (for example, the "current" year), but it also means "a flow of water (or air)." If you think about it, you will see that money and water behave in similar ways: they are both are essential for wealth and their nature is to flow; when not moving they degrade (water stagnates/money loses value); but when they are invested, they generate prosperity and growth (water nurtures crops and trees/money yields interest).

In Feng Shui, **water symbolically represents money**:

- Water flowing **towards** the front of the house means money coming in

- Water flowing **away** from the front of the house means money that never quite reaches us

- Water in the **back** yard represents money that was lost in the past (and every moment that passes becomes part of the past, this can be translated to continually losing money)

So if you want to have a pond or a fountain, it is best to place them by the front door **if you have a sunny entrance.** If your entrance is shady most of the day during a large part of the year, avoid having water by it.

If you have a shady entrance you can have a pond or fountain in your front yard, but it should be far enough from the home that the building doesn't cast a shadow on it all the time. Water fountains should always have the water flow in the direction of the front door.

6.4.1 WATER INSIDE THE HOME

What about pools?

For reasons of space and privacy, most pools are located in the back yard and in strict Feng Shui terms this would translate into a loss of money. **Solution**: This condition can be easily cured by placing two light posts (or spot lights) behind the two back corners of the pool, pointing towards the center of the building's roof.

What about houses that face a road, but have a body of water behind them?

In the Western world it has become fashionable to have a house with a lake or other water source at the back, but this is bad Feng Shui. **Solution**: Place two light posts or spot lights at the back corners of your property, pointing towards the center of the building's roof.

Water fountains and images of waterfalls are largely used in Feng Shui to attract money. Water flowing constantly reminds us of the nurturing quality of water and of the abundance that comes with it.

If you were swimming in a river facing in the direction the water is coming from (up river) everything the river carries seems to be brought to you, but if you are facing down river, everything the river carries it carries away from you. Remember this when placing water fountains or waterfall images in the home. These should be located close to the entrance of the home and the direction of the water should point towards the inside of the home so it seems that this water is constantly bringing the blessings of abundance to you. Never place water in a way that it seems to be taking these blessings away from you, towards an outside door.

Do not place water fountains in bedrooms — you may find you get up to go to the bathroom a lot more during the night!

Do not place water fountains in kitchens or close to kitchens — they might give you the impression of having a leak.

Waterfalls are said to bring abundance, but they need to be on the wall that holds the main entrance, so it looks like the water is coming in the home.

Regulate the flow and sound of a water fountain so that it is pleasant. It wouldn't be auspicious to have a fountain that resembles the sound of an open faucet or of a leaky faucet.

Waterfall images are best near the front door, actually sharing the wall where the front door is located. The best waterfall images are those that look like the water is coming right at you. If there is a little bit of a slant in the way the water flows, make sure that it doesn't point to the door but away from it.

6.4.2 PROBLEMS WITH WATER INSIDE THE HOME

- Water being **flushed** away, flushes away money. Acquire the habit of always putting the toilet seat down before you flush. This is recommended for Feng Shui and sanitary reasons. (Water from a toilet flushing has been found to splatter mini drops in a radius of 25 ft.)

- Water **leaking** translates as a constant escape of wealth, the bigger the leak, the greater the loss. Fix any leaks RIGHT AWAY!

6.5 TAP WATER

The human body is over 70% water, so it is very important that you consume water that is clean. Water can contain organic and inorganic contaminants some of which occur naturally and others which occur due to pollution and even some which are added by the water supply companies (e.g. chlorine for control of bacteria, and the controversial addition of fluoride).

Find out about the quality of water in your area and take the necessary steps to make sure you and your family drink clean, unpolluted water.

The quality of the water in the United States, where I live, has come into question at different times and for various reasons. We have had a whole house filter installed, plus an under the sink filter that also feeds the refrigerator's ice maker. These filters eliminate or reduce heavy metals, bacteria, and other common pollutants, while leaving some minerals and their electrolytes in our water. In addition to that we have a fluoride reducing carafe that we use for drinking (or cooking) water.

Remember that if your dump something in your water you will end up drinking it, sooner or later. Switch to natural and phosphate free house cleaners and detergents. This way you and your loved ones will be exposed to less harmful chemicals and you'll do your part to protect the larger environment.

Because in Feng Shui money is closely related to water, it can be a good practice to filter water before it comes into your home and being mindful of what you put into the water before it leaves your home, to clear negative issues with money.

6.5.1 WHAT SHOULD WATER BE LIKE?

Drinking water should be neutral or slightly alkaline, (a ph of 7 to 8.5 are considered OK drinking water, though 8.5 would be "hard water"). Distilled water or reverse osmosis water have pH values under 7 and therefore are considered acidic. They can dehydrate and leech minerals from the body. (Wrestlers drink distilled water when they need to "make weight' for matches.)

6.5.2 WHAT NEEDS TO BE IN OUR WATER?

A certain mineral content is necessary in our water. Water is one of the ways in which colloidal trace minerals get into our bodies. Trace minerals are needed by our bodies in minute amounts and they help in a multitude of metabolic functions (examples: chromium, copper, iodine, selenium, etc.) The presence of minerals in the water also brings with it electrolytes. Electrolytes are any substances containing free ions that behave as electrically conductive mediums. The primary ions of electrolytes are sodium, potassium, calcium, magnesium, chloride and a few others. Electrolytes control the balance between the intracellular and extra-cellular environments of our bodies. They affect and regulate the hydration of the body, blood pH, and are critical for nerve and muscle function.

6.5.3 WHAT SHOULD WE REMOVE FROM OUR WATER?

Bacteria; chlorine; heavy metals, lead and mercury in particular; aluminum; pesticides and fertilizers; traces of medications, including contraceptive pills.

I also remove fluoride from our drinking water. Water districts in the US add fluoride to tap water with the intent to improve dental health, however fluoride is toxic. You need to do your own research and make your own informed decision.

6.5.4 WATER FILTERS

Unless you are absolutely sure that the tap water in your home is safe to drink, it would be a good idea to do some research on water filters. Which kind of filter to use depends on your definition of clean water and what the contaminants that you are most concerned with are.

I like to give people who take my classes and workshops this challenge: Make the water that comes out of your home overall cleaner than that which comes into your home.

This is how I address this challenge:

- I had an ionic exchange whole house filter installed, which also has solid carbon and KDF (copper-zinc material). This filter takes care of heavy metals, chlorine and excess minerals. The system we have uses potassium to soften our water (potassium is much better for people and the environment than sodium).

- We have another solid carbon filter installed under the sink. This filter takes care of bacteria that may be present in the pipes inside our home.

- We also have a fluoride reducing carafe which uses alumina, carbon and bone char.

- We use only environmentally friendly cleaners, soaps and shampoos.

I do not drink distilled or reverse osmosis water because it lacks minerals and the necessary electrolytes.

If having a system as complete as above was not an option this is the minimum I would do:

- I would still have the solid carbon, alumina and bone char fluoride reducing carafe.

- I would add chlorine-reducing point of use filters in all showers or at least one and use only that shower.

- I would add a teaspoon of ascorbic acid to bath water (stir with a wooden spoon, not the hand) to neutralize chlorine.

6.6 SYMBOLS OF NATURE

It has only been a handful of generations in industrialized countries and major cities that people live so disconnected from nature that they rarely get fresh air or sunshine. Recently, an emotional disorder – nature deficit disorder – has been identified for city dwellers having to do with being disconnected from nature.

6.6.1 A PLACE WHERE YOU MAY THRIVE

If you were thinking of buying a house, you would drive around the neighborhood for signs of prosperity and safety:

- Carefully landscaped yards, rocking chairs in the front porch, children riding their bikes, etc., would be indications of its being a good neighborhood to raise a family, where people care for and respect each other and like to socialize.

- Dilapidated fences, boarded-up windows, trash on the sidewalks would indicate the neighbors care little for their own property or how others view them.

When societies lived a more natural life we regarded the presence of certain elements as necessary for survival: water, controlled fire, game and fish, abundant vegetation and the fruits of the earth. Even though many of us don't live in communion with nature anymore, we still feel the need to be surrounded by those elements, or by symbols that represent them.

In the home we can also surround ourselves with the symbols of thriving life through the use of artwork, ornaments, and objects from nature.

6.6.2 ARTWORK

Artwork or posters that depict serene, peaceful and beautiful images from nature is preferred. Artwork that represents healthy human interaction or that depicts beautiful animals or objects is also welcome in Feng Shui.

However, artwork that depicts suffering, distorted human or animal figures, violence, aggressive sharp lines, etc. is not Feng Shui correct. This doesn't mean that all abstract or modern art is out in Feng Shui. Abstract art of soft shapes and harmonious colors is alright, it is just abstract art that is violent or confusing that is not recommended. If you have doubts

Artwork as windows

Flowers, birds, water, and sky... all homes can benefit from adding images of thriving nature to their walls.

These images are reproductions from original paintings created by the author for Feng Shui purposes

77

on whether a piece of artwork is Feng Shui correct, ask yourself if this piece would scare a child. If the answer is "yes" then it is better that you let that go.

Rooms with no windows benefit greatly from artwork that depicts the views you might see outside a window — mainly gardens and landscapes.

6.6.3 ORNAMENTS

The main characteristic for Feng Shui correct ornaments is that they not pose a physical threat for people or animals. No sharp corners or anything else that would be potentially harmful. This applies to the object itself but also to the shelves or tables where they are displayed.

Fragile ornaments should only be displayed in places where they are going to be protected and safe.

Live only with the objects that you love. If someone gives you something you don't like let go of it as soon as you can. It is better to be honest with friends and relatives and perhaps have an uncomfortable moment, than to have in your home reminders of a dysfunctional relationship for a long period of time. Displaying a gift that you hate shows indeed you have a dysfunctional relationship with the person who gave it to you.

6.6.4 OBJECTS FROM NATURE

There is much discussion in Feng Shui about the convenience or inconvenience of bringing objects found in nature into the home.

Objects from nature are a great addition to the Feng Shui of a home, as long as they are life affirming.

Rocks and pine cones are great for the home. Crystals are also good. An important consideration when choosing objects of nature to display in the home is the size. Small objects that a toddler might choke on are not considered Feng Shui OK, even when there are no children present, unless they are displayed in a container that is not in the reach of children.

Dead insects or embalmed animals are not acceptable. Furs on the other hand, are Feng Shui correct, though many people today would rather use faux fur because of compassion towards the animal world.

6.6.5 PLANTS

Plants should be healthy and thriving. Broad and rounded leaf plants are preferred in Feng Shui. Droopy plants are to be avoided, as well as plants with negative connotations (e.g. spider plants, mother in law's tongue, etc.). Cactuses are generally not allowed in Feng Shui.

If you don't have a green thumb, it is best you get silk plants or paintings and posters of plants. Dried plants are a no/no in Feng Shui, as they carry with them the energy of decay.

6.6.6 FLOWERS

Live flowers, fresh flowers and silk flowers are great, but dry flowers are not, as they carry the energy of death.

6.6.7 ANIMALS

Your animals should be healthy and thriving. They should also be loved. Make sure pets are well taken care of and respected and that their needs are met.

If you are unable to care for a pet, bring in the energy of the animal kingdom through artwork or ornaments.

Animals that pose a potential danger or are historically associated with danger should be avoided; e.g. pet tarantulas, snakes, etc.

6.6.8 OBJECTS FROM THE SEA

Sea shells are OK because they are merely the former homes of sea life, but sea horses and starfish are not, because they are the dead bodies of sea animals.

Fish were one of the first sources of food for humankind, even before agriculture. Living nearby a body of water holding abundant fish was a big plus for survival. Although fishing for food is not an everyday practice for most people anymore, especially those who live in cities, we all still relate to the existence of abundant fish as a sign of prosperity.

- **Live** fish signify **flow** (of cash among other things), therefore they or their images are good close to the main door.

- **Caught** fish signify **food** and prosperity, and their images are appropriate for the area of the house corresponding to wealth. (See Step 8)

Fresh and silk flowers are good.

Dried flowers are not recommended in Feng Shui.

Shells, former homes of sea animals, are Feng Shui correct,.

Photos or paintings of sea horses and starfish are OK, but NO actual sea horses or starfish should be kept in the home.

Many of my holistic friends have switched to, and campaign for, compact fluorescent light bulbs to replace incandescent bulbs.

Though it is true that compact fluorescent bulbs use considerably less energy than incandescent bulbs and thus help conserve energy, they come with many problems of their own. For one, they work with mercury and mercury vapors, so they need to be disposed of in special ways, that many people may not follow. If one of them breaks, then you are dealing with toxic waste.

From the Feng Shui viewpoint, there are other problems. CFs usually have a spectrum of light that changes color perception and makes skin tones look unhealthy, so in this sense your mirrors and the faces of your loved ones give you a wrong feedback of lack of vitality. This problem can be corrected if you get full spectrum CFs.

Another problem with fluorescent lights is that they flicker in a way that may not be directly visible but that your eyes and brain do pick up and which may be the reason why some people claim to get headaches when exposed to fluorescent lights.

A better alternative than fluorescent light bulbs are LED (light emitting diode) bulbs, which are even more energy efficient than fluorescents and pose no environmental hazards, while producing pleasant lighting effects.

6.6.9 BUGS

Unless you live in a very natural environment without clear limits between the inside and outside of the home or in a place so cold that insects don't thrive, at some moment you will have to face the question of pest deterrents or bug control. When you choose a pest control company try to choose a "green" business that will not spray where it is not necessary, that will use bug specific insecticides, non-toxic to pets and humans when possible, and that all precautions are taken to keep people and animals safe and your yard free of poisons. If your home is regularly sprayed for bugs, it is very important that you have an abundance of house plants or a good air purifier.

Remember that whatever poisons are sprayed inside or outside your home you will very likely breathe them in, so be careful. Do some research about natural ways to deal with insects in the area where you live. For example, I have found that red pepper and peppermint oil are good ant deterrents.

6.7 LIGHTS

It is important that you encourage natural light as much as possible in your home, especially in the winter months.

In the summer, open curtains and blinds on the sides of the home that are not receiving direct sunlight, and keep them drawn, except for short periods of time, on sun facing windows. In the winter, do the opposite, open curtains and blinds on the windows that receive direct sunlight, and keep them drawn on the ones that don't. This way you will get the benefits of natural light while conserving energy.

White, full spectrum and yellow light bulbs are preferred in Feng Shui, as they most closely resemble natural light. Blue lights (like most fluorescents) are not encouraged. (see side box)

It is desirable to have light sources at a minimum of two different heights and two different intensities in every room of the home. For example in the bedroom you may have overhead lights and night table lamps. In the family room you may have table lamps, stand up lamps and an overhead light. Overhead lights are a must in every room.

6.8 SOUNDS

In our modern world there are plenty of noises in our environment, and most of these noises are not pleasant: refrigerators, dishwashers, cars passing by, buzzing electronics, etc.

Hibernate, turn off or unplug electronics that you are not currently using, to reduce the noise level (as well as the electromagnetic emissions).

Incorporate into your home sources of sound that make you feel relaxed or uplifted. For many people the obvious choice is music. For others, recordings of natural sounds — waves, leaves ruffling with the wind, birds — work better. Some new age music combines both. Music can make you sink deeper into a mood or can get you out of it.

When you feel upset, nervous or restless, listen to soft relaxing music, if you are feeling blue, listen to happy tunes, such as dance music.

6.9 PHOTOGRAPHS

Photographs send out very powerful symbolic messages. They give us a great deal of information about a person's values, beliefs and relationships. We can use photographs to give ourselves the kind of feedback that will nurture positive views about ourselves and those with whom we share our lives.

6.9.1 PHOTOGRAPHIC CURES FOR THE DIFFERENT LIFE AREAS

(for location of the Life Areas, check pages 106-113)

- Career, Life Mission and Individuality Area: If you have already identified your life mission and are practicing it as a career, place a small black and white photo of yourself performing your work. If you know what your path is but haven't been able to follow it thus far or if you still haven't found it, place small photos, black and white work better, of people whose work you admire.

- Marriage, Relationships and Partnership Area: If you are part of a couple place a photo of you and your partner in an oval shaped frame, in order to symbolically smooth out the hard edges. Choose a photo where you both look handsome and happy. You may also create a collection of photos of you both ranging from when you first met until present time. These photos should depict happy moments and act as a reminder of how good things have been and can be in your shared life.

- Family, Health and Community Area: Taking studio group photos of the family at different stages is a good practice and helps give members good feedback and security. Photos of your present family should be bigger and better displayed than photos from your original family (parents, siblings, etc.) as those are part of your past. There should be a similar number of extended family photos from both sides of the family tree.

Display photos of all your children or grandchildren or none at all. Ideally, these should be of the same size and in frames of the same kind, placed in a harmonious arrangement.

For more information on the life areas, please read Step #8

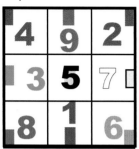

WALL THAT CONTAINS THE FRONT ENTRANCE

1 Career, Life Mission and Individuality

2 Marriage, Relationships and Partnerships

3 Health, Family and Community

4 Wealth, Prosperity and Self Worth

5 Good Fortune Center and Gratitude

6 Helpful People, Travel and Spirituality

7 Children, Creativity and Fun

8 Wisdom, Self Knowledge and Rest

9 Fame, Reputation and Social Life

When displaying individual photos of children or grandchildren, these should be of the same size and be placed in frames that look alike, to promote feelings of equality and avoid giving out the impression of playing favorites.

Make sure that any photos of your present family that are displayed meet the approval of those portrayed in them. A mother may think that a nude baby photo of her child is the cutest thing, while it may become a source of constant embarrassment for the child when he or she reaches school age.

People who have been raised by abusive or overbearing parents or guardians may feel tempted to keep no photos of them at their place. This might work against them, as then the parent or guardian could become a ghostly presence casting a shadow over all areas of life. Displaying a small photo (no bigger than 3 x 4") in an oval or heart shaped frame in the family area of the home helps keep an adequate perspective as to the role they have placed in a person's life. They are part of this area only, and their power over the person is part of the past.

- Wealth, Prosperity and Self Worth: In this area place individual photos of yourself that depict events and achievements that you are proud of and value greatly. You can also place photographs of your dream house, car, boat or any other material possessions you would like to acquire.

If as a child you were made to feel that you where not good enough, place a happy photo of yourself as a four or five year old in a frame that meant luxury to you at that age.

- Center of Good Fortune and Gratitude: Place photographs of special events that remind you of all you are grateful for.

- Helpful People, Travel and Spiritual Connections: Place photographs of teachers and mentors and photos of the places you would like to visit.

- Wisdom, Self Knowledge and Calm: It is better to keep no personal photographs here, but rather images of nature that convey stillness and quiet, especially of mountains.

- Fame, Reputation and Social Life: Place photographs of those achievements that you would like your community to know about, especially images that would look good when presented to the public or to business associates.

6.10 MIRRORS

Mirrors have many uses in Feng Shui. They can serve as chi enhancers or help compensate for yin/yang imbalances or correct disharmonies. They can redirect and disperse negative energy and increase the sense of safety in a room.

- Bagua Mirrors: These small mirrors are octagonal in shape and may or may not have the inscription of the eight trigrams on the outside. They are used to deflect and disperse negative chi in the eight directions. This is a protection mirror that is usually placed above the main door or facing the direction where the negative chi is coming from. If you place a bagua mirror always remember to say a prayer that it is for your protection and that you do not wish anybody harm.

- Convex Mirrors: Are used for security purposes. In stores they are used for surveillance. They can also be used to avoid collisions where two hallways meet at 90 degree or smaller angles. Convex mirrors are good when they reflect general areas. Never place a convex mirror at a height where people can see their faces in it directly, as the image coming back at them will be distorted.

- Big mirrors alongside a wall can visually enlarge a narrow or small space.

- A mirror above the mantelpiece of a fireplace can help compensate for the excess of fire energy.

- A large mirror can visually complete a missing area of a floor plan from the inside, as seen in Step 1.

- Use mirrors to duplicate anything that is good or beautiful, for example, a big mirror in the dining room symbolically doubles up the amount of food, a mirror by the cash register visually duplicates the amount of money coming in.

- Mirrors can be used to allow people a view of the door from the bed or the desk when the power position is not possible, as you will see in Step 9.

A Feng Shui A Feng Shui Cure to Replace the Bagua Mirror

The Sun Bagua Cure works better than the Feng Shui bagua mirror, because it only blesses and protects the building where you place it. It does not harm any other buildings or vehicles nearby.

How to Use a Feng Shui Sun Bagua Cure

Use the **Feng Shui Sun Bagua Cure** in the same manner as the Feng Shui Bagua Mirror. Place the sun right above the beam over the main entrance of your building, on the outside. This is a ceramic ornament. You can use a nail, or you can use strong double sided mounting tape.

Say a prayer when putting up this cure:

I am like a Sun, the Light of God radiates outwards from the Core of my Being outwards in all directions, embracing everyone and everything I love. I send out Only Love and attract Only Good Things. Less-than-love frequencies get consumed by this Fire of Love, recycled and transmuted for Highest Good, long before they ever reach me. I am Love. I am Peaceful. I am Safe.

cafepress.com/fengshuicures.451470662

More tips about mirrors:

- For mirror size, follow the guidelines of traditional photography, so as not to visually "cut" the body in odd places:

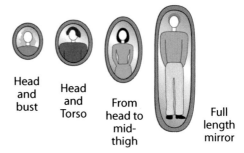

Head and bust · Head and Torso · From head to mid-thigh · Full length mirror

- In bedrooms and other private rooms, such as a home office or study, hang mirrors at a height that allows one of the above views for the person who uses that room the most.

- In shared areas, make sure that no mirrors are "cutting heads off" like in these drawings:

When mirrors meet at 90 degrees strange images result, if you look at yourself in the corner you will see your image is missing the nose and part of the mouth. This gives terrible feedback to a person. You can place leafy plants or an ornament in the corner to cover it up, but it is better to have both mirrors start a few inches away from the corner as in the pictures below. Framed mirrors are better than mirrors with exposed edges.

The two photos at the top of the next page are good examples of how to use mirrors on walls at 90°. The one on the right is better, because the mirrors are framed.

Traditional three pane mirrors on dressers had frames around them and were joined by hinges. These were a great resource to get better views of the self. Our modern bathroom versions though have two major problems associated with them.

First, they usually don't have frames, and even if the edge was been buffed, the unconscious mind will always perceive these as potential sources of danger, as if it was sharp glass.

Second, they meet together in a line and when you see yourself in these you see a split image of yourself at best and sometimes you see the center part of you missing.

Double mirrored doors with no frames around them project back an image split down the middle.

It is best to avoid any mirrors that reflect back odd images, like the ones below:

Fragmented mirrors are very negative. Either remove them or cover them up. This includes tile and mosaic mirrors, as well as those that split up the image. Never hang up any mirrors that distort the image in any way. See how disturbing this outdoors image is, now imagine what it would feel like to see yourself every day in a wall full of fragmented mirrors.

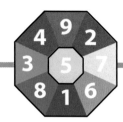

Feng Shui Your Own Home: Key #3

Please answer the questions and follow the instruction in the corresponding sections of the book in the order they are presented. When you are done with each task, please come back to this key and go to the next question.

1. Are all items in your home in good condition and working properly?
   □ Yes   Go to the next question
   □ No   Go to item #7.1 to learn about the importance of taking care of the physical needs of your home.

2. Go to item #7.1.2 to check for repair issues that are especially important in Feng Shui.

3. Are you planning on buying a home where other people have lived before?
   □ Yes   Go to item #7.1.3 to learn how to identify the signs of a healthy home (a home that has been loved and properly taken care of) in the physical level, and go to item 7.3 to learn how to check for energetic health.
   □ No   Go to the next question

4. Do you have a clutter problem?
   □ Yes   Go to item #7.2
   □ No   Go to the next question

5. Would you like to learn an easy method to put a chaotic room in order?

☐ Yes   Go to item #7.2.4
☐ No   Go to the next question

6. Would you like to learn how to keep a place organized after the initial decluttering?

☐ Yes   Go to item #7.2.5
☐ No   Go to the next question

7. Go to item #7.3.1 to learn how to clear a space energetically.

8. Go to Step # 8 to learn about the Feng Shui life areas.

9. Go to item #8.1 to learn how to map the life areas in your home and to identify the 9 points where the life areas are strongest (4 corners, 4 midpoints and the center).

10. Got to item #8.1.1 if you have an attached garage and would like to know whether to include it in the life areas map or not.

11. Go to item #8.2 to see if any of the 9 points where the life areas are strongest in your home are in yin (negative) rooms or spots. Here you will also learn how to project these points to yang (positive) areas.

12 Does your home have more than one story?

☐ Yes   Go to item #8.3
☐ No   Go to the next question

13. Are you confused as to which door in your home is considered your main entrance?

☐ Yes   **Go to item #8.4**

☐ No   **Go to the next question**

14. Do you want to learn the theory behind the way we orient the life areas in the 9 steps to Feng Shui® System?

☐ Yes   **Go to item #8.4.1**

☐ No   **Go to the next question**

15. Go to item #8.5 to learn how to choose a "cure" or enhancement for each life area.

16. Go to item #8.6 and read before you actually decide on cures for the life areas. Then go to item 8.7.

17. Go to items #8.10 and #8.10.1 to see how the life areas relate to different rooms in the home and to find out what kind of "mood" or atmosphere you should seek in each room to be in alignment with Feng Shui purposes.

18. Check items #9.2 and 9.3 to learn about the basic guidelines for furniture choices and placement in Feng Shui.

19. Go to items #9.4, 9.4.1, 9.4.2, 9.4.3 to learn how to place beds and desks in the best location in a room.

20. Go to item #9.4.4 to find out if your bed or desk are in the Feng Shui "danger zone" of a room, and what to do if you cannot move these to a better position.

21. Have you already learned about the power position but find that there is no good placement for the bed other than with a window behind the headboard?

☐ Yes   Go to item #9.4.5

☐ No   Go to the next question

22. Go to item #9.5 to check out more "dos" and "don'ts" of furniture placement.

By this time, if you followed the keys and addressed the questions in the order that they were presented, your home will have great Feng Shui!

Feng Shui for Us™

FSFUS

Nine Steps to Feng Shui
SECURITY • HARMONY • POWER

THE BA-GUA (LIFE AREAS) MAP ON THE MAGIC SQUARE

WEALTH, PROSPERITY AND SELF-WORTH — 4

ELEMENT: WOOD

KEY WORDS/SYMBOLS: PENETRATION, PERSISTENCE, WORTH, DESERVING, HIP

TYPE OF CHI ENERGY: "The Gentle", Wind, Late Spring, 9am-12 Noon, Rising

COLORS: PURPLE, GREEN, GOLD

ENHANCE WITH: Healthy plants, images of material goals, small rocks and crystals, precious metals and stones, soft light sources, luxurious fabrics.

AVOID: Metallic objects, excessive white, red or fire symbols.

LOCATION:
Conscious: Kitchen
Unconscious: Left/Back Corner

FAME, REPUTATION & SOCIAL LIFE — 9

ELEMENT: FIRE

KEY WORDS: INTEGRITY, MAGNIFICENCE, PROPRIETY, EXPOSURE

TYPE OF CHI ENERGY: "The Clinging", Early Summer, 12 Noon-3pm, Radiating, Growth, Sun. **COLORS:** RED, BRIGHT ORANGE

ENHANCE WITH: Candles, lamps, images of people and animals, birds, the sun, symbols of achievement, awards.

AVOID: Water, colors blue and black, organic shapes, waves.

LOCATION: Conscious: Family Room.
Unconscious: Midsection of the Back Wall.

MARRIAGE, RELATIONSHIPS AND PARTNERSHIPS — 2

ELEMENT: EARTH

KEY WORDS/SYMBOLS: RECEPTIVITY, OBEDIENCE, YIELD, FAITH, WOMB

TYPE OF CHI ENERGY: "The Receptive", Earth, Late Summer, 3pm-6pm, Nourishment.

COLORS: PINK, SKIN & EARTH TONES.

ENHANCE WITH: Pairs: two doves, two swans, two roses, etc., images of loving couples, images of gardens, soft and sensual fabrics, cozy furniture.

AVOID: TV, religious images, family photos

LOCATION:
Conscious: Master Bedroom
Unconscious: Right/Back Corner

HEALTH, FAMILY AND COMMUNITY — 3

ELEMENT: WOOD

KEY WORDS/SYMBOLS: STRENGTH, PROGRESS, BENEVOLENCE, FOOT

TYPE OF CHI ENERGY: "The Arousing", Thunder, Early Spring, 6am-9am, Birth, Rising.

COLORS: ALL SHADES OF GREEN

ENHANCE WITH: Healthy plants, objects from nature, vertical stripes, images of nature, photos of family and friends.

AVOID: Metallic objects, excessive white, red or fire symbols.

LOCATION:
Conscious: Dining Room
Unconscious: Midsection of the Left Wall.

GOOD FORTUNE CENTER — 5

ELEMENT: EARTH

KEY WORDS: THANKFUL, CONFIDENT, TRUSTING

TYPE OF CHI ENERGY: Center, Axis, "Void"

ENHANCE WITH: Ceramic objects, religious symbols, images of agriculture and fruits, flowers.

COLORS: YELLOW, EARTH TONES

AVOID: Excess of metallic objects, plants.

LOCATION: Center of the building.

CHILDREN, CREATIVITY & FUN — 7

ELEMENT: METAL

KEY WORDS/SYMBOLS: JOY, INDULGENCE, CREATIVE FORCES, MOUTH

TYPE OF CHI ENERGY: "The Joyful," Lake, Early Fall, 6pm-9pm, Harvest, Winding Down.

COLORS: WHITE, AND PASTELS

ENHANCE WITH: Images of children, flowers, whimsical and colorful objects, artwork made by children, "casual" furniture

AVOID: Symbols of fire, water elements.

LOCATION:
Conscious: Children's Rooms, Art Studio. Unconscious: Midsection of the Right Wall.

WISDOM, SELF-KNOWLEDGE AND REST — 8

ELEMENT: EARTH

KEY WORDS/SYMBOLS: STILLNESS, PAUSE, COMPLETION, HALT, HAND

TYPE OF CHI ENERGY: "Keeping Still", Mountain, Late Winter, 3am-6am, Superficial Calm but Inner Activity.

COLORS: BLUE-GREEN

ENHANCE WITH: Images of mountains and quiet places, landscapes, books, comfortable seating, welcome mats.

AVOID: Artwork that is too active, plants and clocks.

LOCATION:
Conscious: Study, Home Library
Unconscious: Front/Left Corner.

CAREER, LIFE MISSION & INDIVIDUALITY — 1

ELEMENT: WATER

KEY WORDS/SYMBOLS: DEPTH, RISK, FALL, MOVING WATER, STORE, EAR

TYPE OF CHI ENERGY: "The Abysmal", Early Winter, 12 Midnight-3am, Water. **COLORS:** DARK BLUE, BLACK

ENHANCE WITH: Water fountains, aquariums, images of water or life in the water, especially streams and deep water, welcome mats, wind chimes,

AVOID: Excess of square shapes, ceramics, dryness.

LOCATION: Conscious: Foyer, Lobby, Hallways, Corridors
Unconscious: Midsection of the Front Wall.

HELPFUL PEOPLE, SPIRITUAL LIFE & TRAVEL — 6

ELEMENT: METAL

KEY WORDS/SYMBOLS: SYNCHRONICITY, RECTITUDE, HEAD

TYPE OF CHI ENERGY: "The Creator", Heaven, Sky, Late Fall, 9pm-12 Midnight, Preparation.

COLORS: GRAY, MAUVE

ENHANCE WITH: Religious symbols, angels, souvenirs from trips, images of places you would like to visit, photos of ancestors and teachers, welcome mats, wind chimes, soft light sources.

AVOID: Symbols of fire, water elements

LOCATION:
Conscious: Formal Living Room, Sanctuary, Altar
Unconscious: Front/Right Corner

WALL THAT CONTAINS THE MAIN ENTRANCE

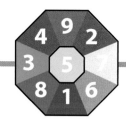

Feng Shui Your Own Home

Step

Fixing and Healing

Maintenance

Decluttering

Clearing

STEP 7: FIXING AND HEALING

HEALING HAPPENS IN 3 LEVELS OF REALITY

Traditional Chinese Thought, which is the basis for both Traditional Chinese Medicine and Feng Shui considers that everything happens in three levels of existence:

• Heaven

• Earth

• Humankind

Heaven deals with the things that are beyond the physical universe and manifest in our minds as thoughts.

Earth is related to the physical world. This three dimensional reality where things require time to take place and where things happen as a response to energy.

Humankind refers to the energy of life, and it manifests as the emotions that motivate human beings to get ideas from Heaven and work on Earth to produce effects in the physical universe. Humans are considered the connectors of heaven and earth.

To keep a home healthy, all three levels need to be addressed.

7.1 KEEP THE GEARS TURNING (EARTH LEVEL)

In the physical universe what doesn't improve gets worse, and maintaining is much better than repairing. Create a maintenance schedule for your home, to make sure you catch problems before they get expensive. Include maintenance for the furnace, air conditioning, water heater and the roof. You may also want to add maintenance schedules to appliances.

7.1.1 ALL ITEMS IN YOUR HOUSE OUGHT TO BE IN GOOD CONDITION AND WORKING PROPERLY

Items that malfunction or do not work at all are easily identified with danger and death. To say the least, they are a sign of deterioration and carelessness. Keeping them is "Bad Feng Shui".

On the other hand, things that are in good condition and working properly are signs of prosperity and unconsciously relate to security and good health.

Functionality does not only apply to proper operation, but also to whether we use them or not. **If we never use them, then they are not working.** If you have items that you have not used for more than a year and one season, you probably do not need them and it may be a good idea to let them go. Either sell them or give them to someone who will use them.

Deterioration and despondency are fast slides on steep hills. Stay on top of this situation. Repair or replace any malfunctioning, broken or torn items as quickly as you can. The longer you wait, the harder it will be, due to loss of momentum. Eventually you may end up getting used to living with them. Every torn or nonworking item is a small source of nuisance. The accumulation of these increases the tensions inside the household and the latter may lead to more arguments.

Take charge. Keep the gears of your home or office turning and running smoothly. You may find that endeavors in other areas of life yield more results, and faster.

7.1.2 TAKE CARE OF THESE OBVIOUS PHYSICAL NEEDS FOR REPAIR, THAT WE SOMETIMES OVERLOOK

- Fix leaks.

- Replace broken glass in windows; the same applies to mirrors.

- Wash or touch-up stains on walls; or paint the whole room or house, if needed.

- Remove stains from carpets and other kinds of floor coverings (or patch them up).

- Glue, nail or tighten bolts and screws on wobbly beds, chairs and tables.

- Make sure all doors and drawers open and close smoothly, fully and noiselessly.

- Have nonworking appliances repaired.

7.1.3 A HEALTHY BUILDING HAS:

- a sound physical structure (foundation, columns, beams, supporting walls, staircases, roof, etc.)

- good condition of the systems (electrical, plumbing, heating, air conditioning, gas lines, etc.)

- proper upkeep and function of elements that open and close, such as doors, windows, cabinet doors and drawers, and that of any built-in elements like closets.

- wall and floor coverings that are clean and properly maintained (paint, wallpaper, carpet, wood, tile, etc.).

The furnishings of a building are also part of the health of a home:

- the furniture, which should be in good condition, comfortable, functional and safe.

- the condition and cleanliness of artwork hanging from the walls, curtains and other kinds of window treatments (like blinds) and that of rugs and mats on the floor.

7.2 DEAL WITH CLUTTER (HUMANKIND LEVEL)

7.2.1 THERE IS NO WAY AROUND CLEANING AND ORGANIZING

During consultations, customers who share their homes or workplaces with messy people frequently ask if there is some kind of "cure" they can use to "override" the other person's clutter or uncleanliness. Unfortunately, there is no such cure.

There is stagnation present in spaces that are cluttered or unclean. When we say something is stagnant, this means it is not moving or flowing, and it then becomes stale, dirty, and foul as a consequence. I am sure all of you have experienced at some point in your lives a sense of relief and a sudden, uplifting, invigorating feeling after performing a simple cleaning or organizing task, such as washing the windows in your house or cleaning up a drawer or closet.

Keep your space free of clutter. Your choices and habits define your environment and your surroundings influence your views on yourself and life as well.

- live only with those objects that you use and love, and that give you a positive feeling about yourself, your loved ones and your life

- emphasize comfort and safety when arranging your rooms, get set up with the right kind of furniture, accessories and lighting for the activities you want to perform in that space.

- visit and straighten out storage areas of your home, office or garden at least once every six months (ideally every three months). This includes storage rooms, sheds, closets, high cabinets, attics, finished and unfinished basements.

7.2.2 TIPS FOR DECLUTTERING THE HOUSE

Start in your bedroom or the room you use most often. Then move on to other rooms.

Watch out for the following:

- Things that are obviously and indisputably rubbish (e.g. clothes tags, outdated newspapers, invitations for events that have already taken place, expired coupons, packaging, etc.). Recycle them or throw them away.

- Things that are broken or damaged beyond repair. Throw them away, recycle them or give them to somebody who can use them for spare parts.

- Things that are broken or malfunctioning but can be repaired — fix them or give them to someone who will.

- Things that work fine, but you don't really use—pass them on to someone who needs them, or take them to your church, the Salvation Army, Good Will, thrift store, etc.

- Things you use but don't like because they are too old, uncomfortable, unsafe, or ugly.

- Things you use and like but were given to you by someone who treated you poorly or didn't mean well—make plans to replace them soon.

> As we clean and organize our spaces, we clear and organize our minds.
>
> Housework provides us with wonderful opportunities to quiet the mind and get insights from our higher selves.

- Let go of any other items that evoke negative feelings in you like guilt or resentments, or that bring you bad memories.

- Let go of the things you do not love.

- Let go of the items that no longer represent who you are or who you want to be.

If the task seems too big, start with one object, deal with it, and then choose another object and deal with it. One by one, until you feel more comfortable and secure to handle other chores.

If you have difficulty throwing or giving away things, take an intermediate step: put them in two big cardboard boxes (mark them: "things to recycle or throw away" and "things to give away"). If you find it hard to get the boxes, two heavy duty trash bags will do. These will give you the opportunity of looking through them if you change your mind about a certain object before it leaves your house.

Yard or garage sales are OK as long as they take place fast (within three months of your decision to start decluttering the house), otherwise, you will be better off just giving those objects away.

For especially challenging cases, keep in mind that there are specialized books videos and audio recordings that teach people how to get rid of clutter and become more organized. There are also professionals who clean and organize people's places for a living; they are a great option, for example, when job schedules make it hard for us to perform all the necessary house chores, or when it has become our responsibility to organize someone else's place and we find it hard to confront it emotionally.

- Expect to feel a sensation of emptiness or regret as you rid your place of clutter. This is natural. In a short time, this process will reduce your tendencies to give in to negative emotions, and you will start feeling better and stronger. Your mind will be clearer and your heart lighter. Remember: you are making room for chi, the life force to run more freely through the different spaces of your home and this will create better conditions for a thriving life.

7.2.3 HEALING AND CLEANSING

During true healing processes, the body expels toxins from top to bottom, inside-out, and from back to front.

Follow the same guidelines when cleaning the house.

Start organizing drawers and cabinets, then closets, then the bedroom you sleep in, the other bedrooms in the house, the bathroom, then the home office if you have one, then the kitchen, living and dining areas. Then tackle outside storage rooms, garages, and carports.

7.2.4. CHAOTIC ACTIVE SPACE

This relates to messiness in an area you use regularly. We are talking extreme chaos here. You find it hard to even get into the room, but yet you have to because this is where you work, or where you sleep.

A chaotic room indicates a state of confusion, and this is how you tackle it:

1) Stand in the middle of the room, look around you on the floor and pick up ONE item that is indisputably trash. Put it in a bag or box labeled "trash." Stand up in the middle of the room again and repeat the procedure. Do this up to seventeen times.

2) Then, stand in the middle of the room, look around you, giving special attention to shelves, tables and dressers. Identify ONE object that is broken, torn or damaged beyond the possibility of repair. Put it in a bag or box labeled: "broken beyond fixing." Stand in the middle of the room again and repeat the procedure. Do this up to thirteen times.

3) Then, stand in the middle of the room and look around you on the floor. Identify ONE item that you LOVE, pick it up and place it safely on a bed or couch. Stand in the middle of the room again and repeat the procedure. Do this up to seventeen times.

4) Then, stand in the middle of the room, look around you, giving special attention to shelves, tables and dressers. Identify ONE object that is OK, but you do not use or do not like and put it in a bag or box labeled "to give away." Stand in the middle of the room again and repeat the procedure. Do this up to thirteen times.

5) Then, stand in the middle of the room, look around you, on the floor and furniture and identify ONE item that no longer represents who you are or who you want to be. Put it in the bag or box labeled "to give away." Stand in the middle of the room again and repeat the procedure. Do this up to nine times.

Repeat steps from 1-5 three times and you should be done. As you go along it will get easier. You can get someone else to coach you while you do this, but it is better that they **don't** physically help you, since your

Buildings seem to have a soul of their own. There are many things we can tell about a home or office upon entering it. Our senses will give us feedback that when contrasted to past experience in the backs of our minds will help us identify the "mood" of the place as happy or sad, cozy or unwelcoming, relaxed or stressed out, tolerant or irritable, rigid or flexible, light or heavy, healthy or ill... We often refer to this general feeling we get from a place as its "atmosphere."

TIP: When you move into a place where something negative has occurred, replace all light bulbs, even if they are still working. This gives you a fresh start and a chance to clean and look at the conditions of light fixtures

attention will be distracted wondering what they are doing, and worrying that they may be throwing away something you want to keep.

7.2.5 PUTTING ONE ROOM IN ORDER

Start by scanning the room and pick up all the "throwables," items that belong in the trash can or recycling bin. Route them to the proper container.

- Scan the room again and locate any items that do not belong in that room. Pick up items one by one and take them to their places [tip: do not fall into the temptation of tidying up the room where you took a certain object, if you do, you will loose your focus.

- Then locate any items that belong to the room but are not in their proper places. Put them back in their places.

- Next straighten out items that even though they are in their proper places, have been moved or look askew.

- What you will be left to deal with then are what I call "undefinable" items. Those objects that have no place, that you are not sure who they belong to, don't know whether to keep them or throw them out or give them away.

- When organizing, start from the floor up.

- When cleaning, start from the top down.

7.3 CLEARING SUBTLE ENERGIES (HEAVEN LEVEL)

Start by checking the energy level, including:

- the state of the health and mood of the people who live or work there

- the state of personal belongings of the occupants of the home

- the general smell of the place

- the condition of live plants and pets... Are they thriving or do they look sickly?

- Is the place cluttered or dirty?

Additionally, inquire about the history of the building itself and that of its previous occupants. Watch out for the following:

A. History of ruptured pipes, short-circuits, invasion of plagues of insects or rodents

B. History of divorce, bankruptcy or violent death in the premises

If you have proof that undesirable or shocking events occurred at a place, or even if without any evidence you have a strong "feeling" that this is the case, you may need to cleanse the energy of such place.

In Feng Shui, we use:

- fire, as in candles, or safely burning alcohol [spirits] in a container,

- penetrating scents such as incense, essential oils, and lemon or pine scented cleaners, and

- vibrating sounds like those produced by bells, gongs, reverberating music, clapping...

...to clear a building from stagnated or sick chi, but the clearing cannot be performed in its entirety if the building is not physically cleaned first, as dust, spills and fouls smelling items will keep sick chi in place. In extreme cases, it is better to let go of any furniture with porous materials that may have absorbed the stagnant energy. If the items must be kept, they should be taken outside and exposed to fresh air and sun while they are being cleaned.

If you can, take all furniture out of a room you are going to clear after an illness or death has occurred there, so that first you can do a "deep" cleansing, with one window and one door open. Once the physical task has been completed, let incense burn (sage is an excellent choice) while you follow the procedure explained in the next two pages.

If you wish, you may enlist the help of a priest, a shaman, or a friend or relative with "excellent luck" to perform the cleansing or clearing of negative chi,.

Odor absorbing agents will also absorb stagnated chi, like a brown paper bag full of charcoal, odor absorbing stones (usually used for basements and which can be reactivated by exposure to the sun) or air purifiers with carbon filters.

7.3.1 USING THE SEVEN ANGELIC HEALING RAYS TO CLEANSE A SPACE

There is something mysterious and powerful in walking through a space while clearing stagnant or sick chi by following the path of the seven rays, which makes the process faster and much more effective than just walking in a random way or in a circular motion.

It is simpler than it looks. In your mind, place the magic numbers in the corners and midpoints of the room and then just follow the numbers (only you begin with "three" instead of "one"): 3 - 4 - 5 - 6 - 7 - 8 - 9 - 1 - 2.

7.3.2 THE CLEANSE

Before you begin, stand outside of the building or room, clap three times to call the attention of Heaven, Earth and Humankind and announce your intention of going inside to perform a cleanse. Enter the space and light some incense (sage works great) on a heat resistant surface close to the middle of the room or building. For the cleanse you can carry either a candle , or a big feather (a feather duster will work too) in your right hand.

Starting at the point marked with number "three" think about and visualize the circumstances relating to Family, Health and Community that you would like to change. Accept and give thanks for what is and what you have learned from it, then release all negativity related to that Life Aspiration, cleaning it symbolically with the feather or "consuming" it in the fire., Ask that all that is cleared is replaced by blessings. Now walk to the corner marked with the number "four."

At number "four" follow the same steps as you did at number "three:" visualize, accept, give thanks and release, only this time focus your attention on "Wealth, Prosperity and Self Worth." Then walk to number "five" and pause there briefly, breath deeply and exhale three times. Say a prayer of gratitude if you wish. Continue to number "six"

At number "six," visualize, accept, give thanks and release matters related to "Helpful People, Travel and Spirituality." Then walk to number "seven."

At number "seven" do the same for "Children, Creativity and Fun. "Walk to number "eight."

At number "eight" do the same for "Wisdom, Self-Knowledge and Stillness" Go to number "nine."

At number "nine" do the same for "Fame, Reputation and Social Life." Walk to number "one."

At number "one" do the same for "Career, Life Mission and Individuality." Then walk to number "2".

At number "two" do the same for "Relationships, Partnerships and Marriage" Then walk to the back door if there is one or go back to the front door. Before you leave, declare that you are done doing the cleanse and that all negativity in the room was either consumed by the fire or "trapped" in the feather.

Then walk to the back door if there is one or go back to the front door. Before you leave, declare that you are done with the blessing and than when you blow out the candle all the good intentions and your prayers remain in the room or building. Then exit.

Walk outside. If using a candle, let it burn out completely (please take all precautions); if using a feather wash it with abundant water (and soap if you wish).

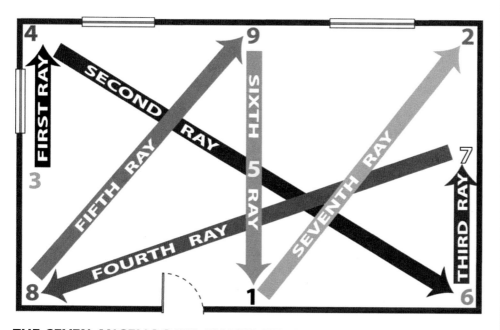

THE SEVEN ANGELIC RAYS ON THE FENG SHUI CLEARING PATTERN

WHAT THE SEVEN ANGELIC HEALING RAYS ARE ABOUT

First Ray:
Will or Power

Second Ray:
Love, Wisdom

Third Ray:
Active Intelligence

Fourth Ray:
Harmony, Beauty, Art

Fifth Ray:
Science

Sixth Ray:
Devotion, Idealism

Seventh Ray:
Ceremonial Order

The healing rays come from the Western Tradition of Alchemism.

There is no known connection between the meanings of the seven rays and the Life Aspirations. It is the pattern that their sequence creates when combined with the Magic Square that is of use in Feng Shui.

Incense,
candles,
feathers,
sage,
bells,
alcohol,
salt...
some of the tools
you can use to clear
stagnant chi.

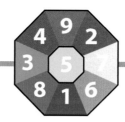

Feng Shui Your Own Home

Step

Assigning and Enhancing the Life Areas

There are four corners and midpoints in a home that correspond with our mental, physical and emotional associations to the different areas of our lives.
If we learn to recognize these we can work with them to identify problems in the way we relate to life and to place reminders of our goals in key spots where their presence supports our aspirations.

STEP EIGHT: ASSIGNING AND ENHANCING THE LIFE AREAS

ASSIGNING THE LIFE AREAS TO SECTORS IN THE HOME

In order to achieve our full development as human beings, we must devote our attention and efforts to several different aspects of life.

The old Feng Shui masters, through careful observation of human nature, determined these aspects to be:

1. Career, Life Mission and Individuality

2. Marriage, Relationships and Partnerships

3. Health, Family and Community

4. Wealth, Prosperity and Self Worth

5. Center of Good Fortune and Gratitude

6. Spirituality, Helpful People and Travel

7. Children, Creativity and Fun

8. Wisdom, Self Knowledge and Rest

9. Fame, Reputation and Social Life

In Feng Shui we assign each of these lifea areas to sectors of the home.

We divide the home into nine equal squares or rectangles and assign a life area to each according to an arrangement inspired in the Ancient Chinese book of changes called the I-Ching.

The book of changes identifies 8 forces of nature that are symbolic of the different moods and attitudes that are helpful for us when addressing different aspects of life. These forces rotate around a center that is hollow, like the center of a wheel.

These forces of nature are:

1. Water, represented by the gorge

2. Earth, as expressed in the agricultural field

3. Thunder, associated to the blessings of rain and the generating power of lightning.

4. Wind, with its penetrating nature as it breezes through the bamboo forest.

5. The hollow center, or void, around which all of life revolves.

6. Heaven, this includes the sky, outer space and that part of life that goes beyond the physical.

7. Lake, a still and tranquil lake that you enjoy as the sun sets and the chores of the day are complete.

8. Mountain, associated with strength and the ability to see things from above.

9. Fire, which heats up, illuminates, bonds things together and creates passion.

This is how the forces of nature are associated with the Feng Shui Life Areas:

1. Water is for Career, Life Mission and Individuality. Water soaks and goes down. It follows the path of least resistance and at it flows it encounters other sources of water that join it in its path to the ocean. Water doesn't stop when it reaches the edge of a cliff, it creates a beautiful waterfall.

2. Earth (field) is for Marriage, Relationships and Partnerships. The field allows the plowing and then receives the seeds, which it nourishes and helps grow. Earth is receptive and yielding, the energy of a mother.

3. Thunders is for Health, Family and Community. It carries the energy of rain and lightning that trigger the sprouting of plants in the early Spring.

4. Wind is for Wealth, Prosperity and Self Worth. Wind is connected to the life and strength of a tree, which grows in depth, height, and thickness every year.

5. The void, or center is associated with the Center of Good Fortune and Gratitude.

6. Heaven is for Helpful, People, Travel and Spirituality.

7. The Lake is for Children, Creativity and Fun. At the end of the day, when responsibilities have been fulfilled, comes the time to enjoy.

8. The Mountain is for Wisdom, Self Knowledge and Rest. In many cultures of the world you hear of sages going off to the mountains to seek wisdom.

9. Fire is for Fame, Reputation and Social Life. You want your reputation to spread around like a wildfire, and to go up, as is the nature of fire.

When the life areas are applied to a floor plan or bird eye's view of a building, we use a tic-tac-toe pattern.

8.1 HOW TO APPLY THE LIFE AREAS (OR BA-GUA) MAP TO A FLOOR PLAN

The term ba-gua means "eight trigrams." A trigram is a symbol that represents a particular combination of yin (split) and yang (solid) lines. Each one of these symbols represents one of the forces of nature described above. These symbols are combined with a number arrangement called the Magic Square to create the Life Areas Map that is super-imposed over a home's floor plan.

When a home is square or rectangular it is very easy to apply the life areas map to it. Measure one side and divide it in three segments, then do the same for the other side. Now join the points to form a tic-tac-toe and you end up with nine equal squares or rectangles.

This tic-tac-toe determines the sectors for each life area.

Each life area is also designated by a number. On the next page you see a life areas map with some details about each life area, and on page 109 there is the key to the numbers and life areas.

Notice that on this key I have marked the corners and midpoints in each sector. There are four life areas that have corner points and there are four life areas that have midpoints, plus the center, which has its strongest point in the center of the sector as well.

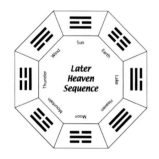

ABOVE: The Ba-gua Symbol

BELOW: The Magic Square. If you add up 3 numbers in any direction,, they always add up to 15.

LIFE AREAS (BAGUA) MAP

WEALTH, PROSPERITY AND SELF-WORTH	FAME, REPUTATION AND SOCIAL LIFE	MARRIAGE, RELATIONSHIPS AND PARTNERSHIPS
ELEMENT: WOOD NUMBER: 4 SEASON: LATE SPRING COLORS: PURPLE AND GREEN	ELEMENT: FIRE NUMBER: 9 SEASON: EARLY SUMMER COLORS: RED, BRIGHT ORANGE, LEMON YELLOW	ELEMENT: EARTH NUMBER: 2 SEASON: LATE SUMMER COLORS: PINK, SKIN TONES, EARTH TONES
HEALTH, FAMILY AND COMMUNITY	CENTER OF GOOD FORTUNE AND GRATITUDE	CHILDREN, CREATIVITY AND FUN
ELEMENT: WOOD NUMBER: 3 SEASON: EARLY SPRING COLORS: ALL SHADES OF GREEN AND LIGHT BLUES	ELEMENT: EARTH NUMBER: 5 SEASON: ALL TRANSITIONS BETWEEN SEASONS COLORS: YELLOW, EARTH TONES	ELEMENT: METAL NUMBER: 7 SEASON: EARLY FALL COLORS: WHITE, PASTEL TONES RAINBOWS
WISDOM, SELF-KNOWLEDGE AND REST	CAREER, LIFE MISSION AND INDIVIDUALITY	HELPFUL PEOPLE SPIRITUAL LIFE AND TRAVEL
ELEMENT: EARTH NUMBER: 8 SEASON: LATE WINTER COLORS: TEAL AND THE COLORS OF MOUNTAINS IN THE DISTANCE	ELEMENT: WATER NUMBER: 1 SEASON: EARLY WINTER COLORS: BLACK, NAVY BLUE AND OTHER VERY DARK COLORS	ELEMENT: METAL NUMBER: 6 SEASON: LATE FALL COLORS: GRAY, MAUVE

WALL THAT HOLDS THE MAIN ENTRANCE

© 2009 MONICA P. CASTANEDA

These corners and midpoints are the places where the energy of the life area is stronger, and the best for placing enhancements related to goals in each life area.

When the floor plan is incomplete, for example an L shape, some life areas or portions may be outside the building. In these cases the building needs to be virtually completed on the outside (see chapter 1). On the inside you need to find another point inside the home that can hold your desires for those life areas. This is called projecting corners and mid-points of the life areas, which we will discuss in more depth later in this chapter.

Each life area works with one of the five elements. Since there are 9 life areas some of the elements repeat.

The graphic on page 110 shows which element rules the energy of each of the life areas, because the element is one of the determining factors when choosing cures for the life areas.

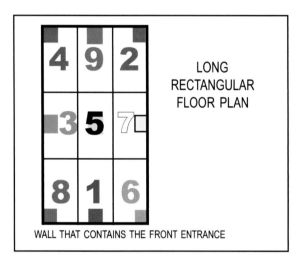

LONG RECTANGULAR FLOOR PLAN

WALL THAT CONTAINS THE FRONT ENTRANCE

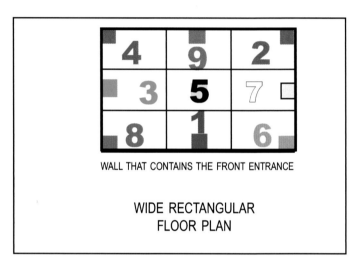

WALL THAT CONTAINS THE FRONT ENTRANCE

WIDE RECTANGULAR FLOOR PLAN

1 Career, Life Mission and Individuality

2 Marriage, Relationships and Partnerships

3 Health, Family and Community

4 Wealth, Prosperity and Self Worth

5 Good Fortune Center and Gratitude

6 Helpful People, Travel and Spirituality

7 Children, Creativity and Fun

8 Wisdom, Self Knowledge and Rest

9 Fame, Reputation and Social Life

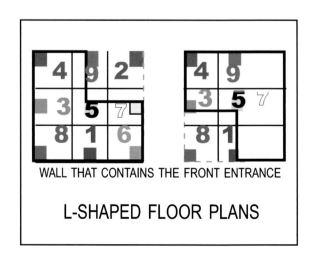

WALL THAT CONTAINS THE FRONT ENTRANCE

L-SHAPED FLOOR PLANS

8.1.1 WHEN TO INCLUDE GARAGES IN THE LIFE AREAS MAP

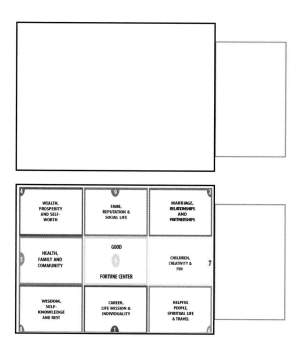

WEALTH, PROSPERITY AND SELF-WORTH	FAME, REPUTATION & SOCIAL LIFE	MARRIAGE, RELATIONSHIPS AND PARTNERSHIPS
HEALTH, FAMILY AND COMMUNITY	GOOD FORTUNE CENTER	CHILDREN, CREATIVITY & FUN
WISDOM, SELF-KNOWLEDGE AND REST	CAREER, LIFE MISSION & INDIVIDUALITY	HELPFUL PEOPLE, SPIRITUAL LIFE & TRAVEL

If the garage is a separate structure attached to one side of the house do not include it in the life areas map.

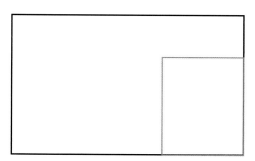

WEALTH, PROSPERITY AND SELF-WORTH	FAME, REPUTATION & SOCIAL LIFE	MARRIAGE, RELATIONSHIPS AND PARTNERSHIPS
HEALTH, FAMILY AND COMMUNITY	GOOD FORTUNE CENTER	CHILDREN, CREATIVITY & FUN
WISDOM, SELF-KNOWLEDGE AND REST	CAREER, LIFE MISSION & INDIVIDUALITY	HELPFUL PEOPLE, SPIRITUAL LIFE & TRAVEL

If the garage shares the structure with the rest of the house or if any part of the house lies behind the garage or if there are rooms on top of the garage, then include it in the life areas map.

THE FIVE ELEMENTS AND THE LIFE AREAS (OR BA-GUA) MAP

4 Wood	9 Fire	2 Earth
3 Wood	5 Earth	7 Metal
8 Earth	1 Water	6 Metal

WALL THAT CONTAINS THE MAIN ENTRANCE

1 Career, Life Mission and Individuality

2 Marriage, Relationships and Partnerships

3 Health, Family and Community

4 Wealth, Prosperity and Self Worth

5 Good Fortune Center and Gratitude

6 Helpful People, Travel and Spirituality

7 Children, Creativity and Fun

8 Wisdom, Self Knowledge and Rest

9 Fame, Reputation and Social Life

8.2 PROJECTING THE LIFE AREAS

In the 9 Steps to Feng Shui System we never enhance a life area in one of what are cold yin spots of a home. These are spaces that for one reason or another cannot consistently attract and concentrate positive chi.

The **yin** rooms/spots of a home are as follows:

- Bathrooms
- Staircases
- Laundry rooms
- Closets
- Storage Areas
- Garages
- Areas outside the building

When a corner, midpoint or the center of the home happen to be in one of the above, we must project that corner, midpoint or center to the closest positive or yang area in the home.

The **yang** rooms/spots in the home are:

- Bedrooms
- Kitchen
- Living areas
- Dining areas
- Foyer
- Hallways

The projection of a corner, midpoint or the center from a yin space to a yang space is done based on closeness and the study of the elements.

The next page shows the application of the life areas or ba-gua map to a floor plan that is complete. This floor plan has a back patio and slabs outside the two other doors, which have not been included in the life areas map, as they are considered extensions to the life areas they are attached to. Extensions are good.

On the other hand covered porches and dens do need to be included in the life areas map. Garages may or may not be included. It depends on whether the garage appears to be part of the home in volume or whether it is attached to one side of the home. (see item #8.1.1).

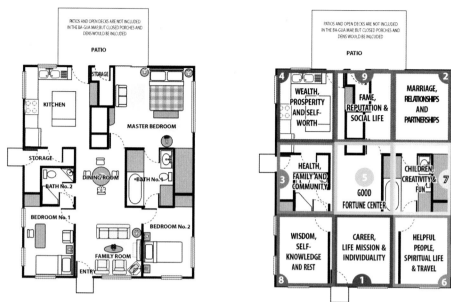

ONE STORY THREE BEDROOM HOME

Here you see a single story three bedroom home. The image above on the left shows the floor plan with the furniture drawn in, while the image on its right shows how the life areas map has been applied to the floor plan. There I have also marked the corners, midpoints and the center.

Notice that there are 3 life areas that have their midpoints located in yin spots of the home.

Life area #3 is located in a bathroom, the same goes

The graphic above shows how to project life areas 3 and 9 out of their previous yin (negative) spots

for life area #7. Life area #9 is in a closet that opens to the outside.

Life area #3 is usually projected, in a case like this, towards life area #4 because these two areas share the same element (wood). But in this particular case the refrigerator is located at the spot where you would do this projection, so instead the midpoint has been projected towards life area #5, and re-located to the outside wall of the bathroom.

In the case of midpoint #7, it has been projected in the direction of life area #6 because they both share the same element (metal).

The midpoint for life area #9 is projected towards life area #2. It could also be projected towards life area #4. I chose to project it to the right, because the next yang spot on this side was closer than on the other side.

All the other midpoints and corners are on yang spots of the home already and do not need to be projected.

On the left sidebar there are some guidelines as to what direction to project the corners and midpoints of the life areas.

THREE BEDROOM HOUSE
with basement (not included)

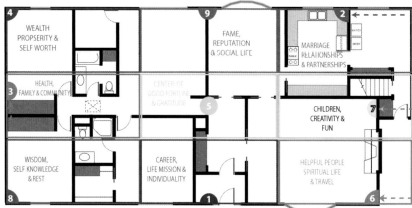

In the page to the left there is an example of a three bedroom house that is missing part of life area #6 and part of life area #7. Both midpoints of these life areas have been projected towards the inside of the home. Life area #2 on the other hand has been projected from the laundry room to a corner in the kitchen. The midpoint of life area #3 has been shifted only slightly to get it out of the closet and into positive space in the room.

8.3 MULTIPLE STORY HOMES

When working with multiple story homes, draw the ba-gua map only on the main floor and then project the life areas to the top or bottom. Project the corners and midpoints as needed. Life area enhancements

TWO STORY HOUSE
plus basement and attic (not shown)

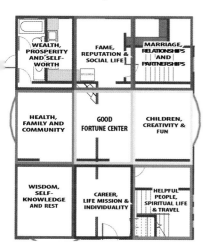
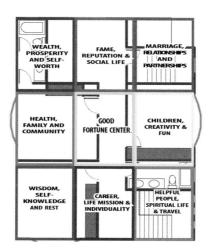

Feng Shui Your Own Home

are usually done on the main floor. It is not necessary to enhance them in all the floors.

In the example in the previous page you would need to project the corner for wealth, prosperity and self worth, life area #4, because it falls in the bathroom. You would also need to project the corner for marriage, relationships and partnerships, life area #2 because that corner is missing.

8.4 THE WALL THAT CONTAINS THE MAIN ENTRANCE

4 Wood	9 Fire	2 Earth
3 Wood	5 Earth	7 Metal
8 Earth	1 Water	6 Metal

WALL THAT CONTAINS THE MAIN ENTRANCE

The front door is the main entrance in most cases. If you use another door a lot more than the front door follow these guidelines:

1.   Where do you get your mail?

2.   Where do private delivery services   drop off packages?

3. If you had guests that were very important to you, which door would you have them use?

If the answer to any of the above questions is "the front door" then you should consider this your main door, even if you mostly use another door.

If you NEVER use your front door, then your side/back/ garage door [the one you use the most] should be considered your main door. Exception: Never assign a back door accessed from an alley as a main door if there is a slope going up from the road to the front door of the house.

8.4.1 WHY DO WE DRAW THE LLIFE AREAS MAP BASED ON THE MAIN ENTRANCE?

The life areas map is based on an octagonal arrangement of natural forces that comes to us from the I-Ching, the ancient Chinese "book of changes," and a "magic square" with an arrangement of numbers that symbolize the representation of each life area. The ba-gua assigns a color to each life area. Each side of the main four sides of the ba-gua octagon on which the ba-gua map is based, has a dominant element, which gives the name to that line. Life Areas 1, 3, 7 and 9 (the midpoints) are lined up parallel

THE FIVE ELEMENTS AND THE LIFE AREAS (OR BA-GUA) MAP

4 Wood	9 Fire	2 Earth
3 Wood	5 Earth	7 Metal
8 Earth	1 Water	6 Metal

WALL THAT CONTAINS THE MAIN ENTRANCE

1 Career, Life Mission and Individuality

2 Marriage, Relationships and Partnerships

3 Health, Family and Community

4 Wealth, Prosperity and Self Worth

5 Good Fortune Center and Gratitude

6 Helpful People, Travel and Spirituality

7 Children, Creativity and Fun

8 Wisdom, Self Knowledge and Rest

9 Fame, Reputation and Social Life

to the line of the corresponding element.

We place Life Area #1 (Career, Life Mission and Individuality) at the front of the building, as this lines it up with the access road or path, which symbolically represents water. We are also placing the "mouth of chi" (main entrance) in line with the pathways that carry the chi currents to the building.

See the graphics at the top of the next page for an example of a property where the front of the building is lined up with the front of the lot and another one were it is not.

8.5 HOW TO CHOOSE A FENG SHUI CURE FOR EACH LIFE AREA

Now that you have learned how to assign the corners and midpoints of the life areas, let's talk about how to enhance these spots so that your life is showered with blessings in each life area.

A Feng Shui cure is intended to help bring in and let us connect with the kind of Chi energy that is required in each area of the house in order to promote the healthy development of each life area.

There are four factors that determine the choice of a cure: the element, the number, the symbology and the color of the life area.

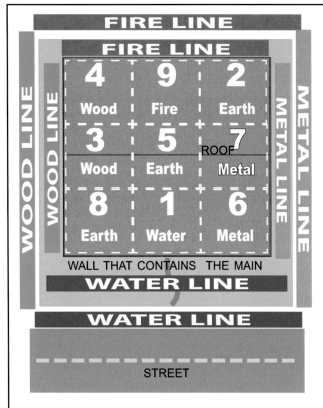

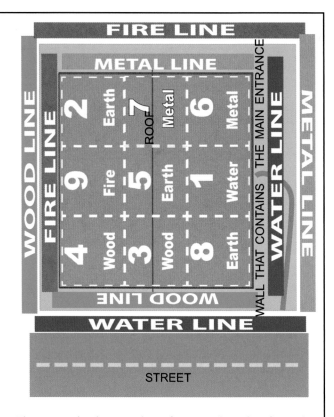

In the birds eye view at the top we have an example of a main door that faces the street.

In this example the element lines for the property coincide with the element lines for the building.

The example above is that of a main door that faces the side of the property. In this case the life areas map has to be turned to align the water of life area #1 with the wall that contains the main entrance, not the wall that faces the street. In this example the element lines for the property are different from those for the building.

1. The element: one of the five elements is assigned to each of the nine life areas. Each element corresponds to certain materials, shapes and colors. So a cure for a specific life area should either have the material, shape or color that represents the element. Ideally, it should have the three (material, shape and color).

ELEMENT	FAMILY OF COLORS	MATERIALS	SHAPES
Wood	Greens	wood, bamboo, natural fibers	tall rectangles, sticks
Fire	Reds	synthetics	pointed, stars, triangles
Earth	Yellows, Browns	ceramic, porcelain, brick	squares, horizontal rectangles
Metal	White, Gray	metals, hard rocks, crystals	circles and spheres
Water	Black, Blues	glass, mirrors	wavy, undulating, oval

2. The life areas numbers have a meaning. For example the number 1 is used for Career, Life Mission and Individuality because this life area refers to the path of life that we usually walk alone, independently of whether or not we are married or have a family. Life area #2, Marriage, Relationships and Partnerships obviously works with the number 2, which represents the couple. The #1 is very destructive for this area because it symbolizes single life and the number 3 is destructive because it symbolizes a love triangle. However, the number 3 is very good for life area #3, Health, Family and Community.

3. Symbology: It is very positive to choose cures that symbolize our cultural and personal aspirations in each Life Area.

4. The color associated with the life area, as shown in the life areas map.

3 Examples of good cures for the life areas:

- A cure for Marriage, Relationships and Partnerships: two pink ceramic hearts. It has the number 2, the color of the life area (pink), the material of the element (ceramic) and a strong symbolic meaning having to do with love.

- A cure for Health, Family and Community: three healthy, tall green plants with long stems. It has the number 3, the color of both the element and the life area, which in this case happens to be the same, the material of the element (plant) and the shape of the tall vertical line in the long stems.

- A cure for Fame, Reputation and Social Life: An image of a red sun with nine flames. It has the number 9 in the nine flames, it is strongly symbolic of fire and the sun which are both representative of this life area, and it has the color red, which represents both the element and the life area.

8.6 THE PRINCIPLE OF "VERY LITTLE"

Before you decide to redecorate your rooms to match the colors, elements or symbols of the Ba-Gua map and the Magic Square, please keep in mind the principle of "very little", less is more.

Small life area enhancements are more effective than aggressive, abrupt, big changes.

Remember that the energy of the life area is strongest around the corner, midpoint or center. In addition, going overboard and doing something like painting a whole room in the color of the life area creates a disharmony of the elements and an imbalance of yin and yang, which are more important in the overall picture of Feng Shui, than life area enhancements.

8.7 HOW TO APPLY FENG SHUI CURES FOR THE LIFE AREAS

A Feng Shui cure for life Areas must have at least two of the following four requirements:

- Be a chi attractor (or chi magnet)

- Honor the number that corresponds to the life area

- Have the color, shape or material of the element (all three much better) for that life area or the color of the life area.

- Have a symbolic meaning in accordance to your own cultural background and belief system.

If you have applied a proper life area cure to a corner or midpoint and after a week you see no sign of improvement, de-clutter the area around the cure within a one foot radius; if another week has passed and you see no results, then de-clutter around the cure within a two feet radius; if you wait another week and still no results, de-clutter around the cure within a three foot radius. If you have done all this and have not seen a sign of improvement in that life area, then check what happens at the other end of the spoke.

If the area opposite that on which you are working is thriving you can take some object from there to the latter to balance out the energy. If both areas are a problem, then proceed as follows:

If 4-6 are problems, then work on 5

If 8-2 are problems, then work on 9

If 3-7 are problems, then work on 5

If 1-9 are problems, work on 4 and 6

WEALTH, PROSPERITY AND SELF-WORTH	FAME, REPUTATION AND SOCIAL LIFE	MARRIAGE, RELATIONSHIPS AND PARTNERSHIPS
ELEMENT: WOOD NUMBER: 4 SEASON: LATE SPRING COLORS: PURPLE AND GREEN	ELEMENT: FIRE NUMBER: 9 SEASON: EARLY SUMMER COLORS: RED, BRIGHT ORANGE, LEMON YELLOW	ELEMENT: EARTH NUMBER: 2 SEASON: LATE SUMMER COLORS: PINK, SKIN TONES, EARTH TONES
HEALTH, FAMILY AND COMMUNITY	CENTER OF GOOD FORTUNE AND GRATITUDE	CHILDREN, CREATIVITY AND FUN
ELEMENT: WOOD NUMBER: 3 SEASON: EARLY SPRING COLORS: ALL SHADES OF GREEN AND LIGHT BLUES	ELEMENT: EARTH NUMBER: 5 SEASON: ALL TRANSITIONS BETWEEN SEASONS COLORS: YELLOW, EARTH TONES	ELEMENT: METAL NUMBER: 7 SEASON: EARLY FALL COLORS: WHITE, PASTEL TONES RAINBOWS
WISDOM, SELF-KNOWLEDGE AND REST	CAREER, LIFE MISSION AND INDIVIDUALITY	HELPFUL PEOPLE SPIRITUAL LIFE AND TRAVEL
ELEMENT: EARTH NUMBER: 8 SEASON: LATE WINTER COLORS: TEAL AND THE COLORS OF MOUNTAINS IN THE DISTANCE	ELEMENT: WATER NUMBER: 1 SEASON: EARLY WINTER COLORS: BLACK, NAVY BLUE AND OTHER VERY DARK COLORS	ELEMENT: METAL NUMBER: 6 SEASON: LATE FALL COLORS: GRAY, MAUVE

WALL THAT HOLDS THE MAIN ENTRANCE

© 2009 MONICA P. CASTANEDA

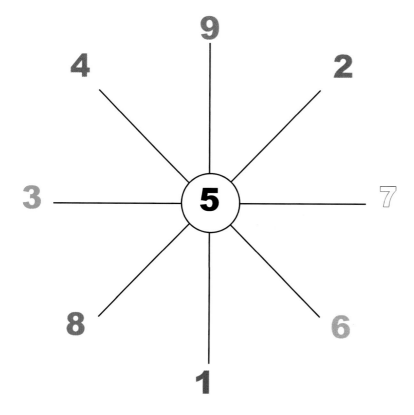

8.9 THE COMBINED MOODS OF THE LIFE AREAS

The graphic below offers more information to understand the energy that is best for each of the life areas. It will help you at the moment of choosing Feng Shui cures or enhancements.

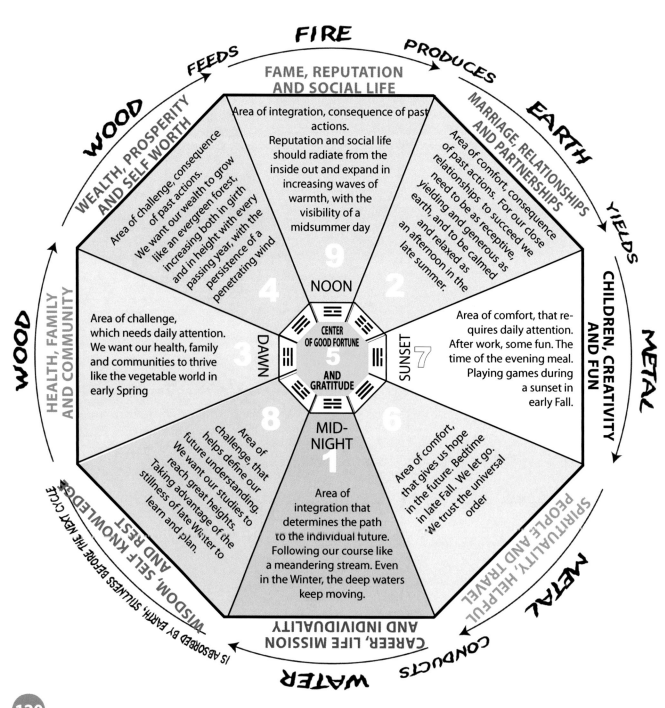

8.10 THE LIFE AREAS ARE ALSO EXPRESSED IN SPECIFIC ROOMS OF THE HOME

The life area corners and midpoints are unconscious to the extent that people don't know what they are until they read about Feng Shui or someone tells them about it.

The rooms of the home, on the other hand, have conscious associations with the life areas. For example, everyone knows that the master bedroom is related to the couple and most people realize that it is during meals that communication with the family tends to happen naturally.

Below is a chart that shows how the different rooms in the home connect with the life areas in Feng Shui:

LIFE ASPIRATIONS	ROOM OR AREA OF THE HOME	MAGIC No
Career, Life Mission and Individuality	Foyer and hallways	1
Marriage, Relationships and Partnerships	Master Bedroom	2
Health, Family and Community	Dining Areas	3
Wealth, Prosperity and Self Worth	Kitchen	4
Spirituality, Helpful People and Travel	Shrines, altars, sacred spaces	6
Children, Creativity and Fun	Children's Rooms. or craft and hobby rooms	7
Wisdom, Self Knowledge and Rest	Study, Home Library, Book Shelves	8
Fame, Reputation and Social Life	Family Room	9

On the next page you will find a chart with advice on what kind of mood to create in each of these rooms to further the right kind of energy that benefits the life area associated with the room. In the chart I have placed the information for each room in the same quadrant as the life area it relates to, but this applies to each room no matter what the location in the home.

8.10.1 KEEP THESE THOUGHTS IN MIND WHEN CHOOSING THE DECOR FOR EACH ROOM

Think royalty, money, jewels, gold, luxury richness, high self esteem, cornucopia, morning, purple, indigo, burgundy, green, fruit, best quality, late spring, abundant natural life, trees, flowers. **KITCHEN**	Think fire, explosion, radiation, power, laughter, summer, kites, balloons, fairs, tan, shine, red, glitter, spotlights, triangles, pyramids, blazing sun, stars, exposure, visibility, outdoor shows. **FAMILY ROOM**	Think tea time in the back porch, holding hands, poetry, fertility, earth, agriculture, pink, couples, walks on the beach, solidarity, stability, receptivity, porcelain, clay, ceramics. **MASTER BEDROOM**
Think spring, sunrise, trees, gardens, new beginnings, life thriving, sprouts, buds, hope, spring fever, flower prints, rain. **DINING AREAS**	Think earth, fertility, field, farming, generosity, yellow, ceramic, clay, squares, low height, ground, dirt, sand. **CENTER OF THE HOME**	Think joy, contentment, play, games, art, mischief, magic, whim, fun, loitering, relaxation, pleasure, babies, childhood, imaginary friends, white and pastel colors. **CHILDREN'S BEDROOMS OR CRAFT/HOBBY ROOMS**
Think mountain, sage, heights, loneliness, peace, studies, mist, fog, sacred space, stillness, meditation, prayer, retreat, withdrawal, monastery, temple. **BOOK SHELVES, STUDY**	Think depths, winter, darkness, new moon, night, mystery, hiding path, black, deep blues, water, organic shapes, waves, plunging, glass, undulation, footprints, yearnings, dreams. **FOYER & HALLWAYS**	Think teachers, mentors, angels, generous friends, travel souvenirs, images of places you would like to visit, religious symbols, metal, crystals, hard rocks (marble, granite), white, gray, mauve. **ALTARS AND OTHER SACRED SPACES**

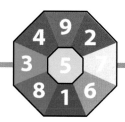

Feng Shui Your Own Home

Step

Furniture Placement

In the same room, with the exact same furniture and accessories, items can be placed in a way that dis-empowers, weakens and distracts people or in a way that empowers them, helping them concentrate and be in control of their surroundings.

In Feng Shui we promote the "Power Position"

STEP NINE: FURNITURE PLACEMENT

In Feng Shui the number nine is the maximum of yang (light, hot, dry and strong), the power to make things happen, to get things done. "Power" is the ability to turn ideas into action or facts. Nine represents the cohesive force that makes couples, families, businesses, partnerships, communities, etc., stick together.

We can arrange our furniture inside of a room to align ourselves with this power which will enable us to achieve the maximum efficiency with the minimum effort. In order to do this, whatever the activity –work, cook, play games, rest or sleep– that is performed in a room, we need to feel comfortable, safe and in control.

9.1 COMFORT

How comfortable a piece of furniture is has less to do with how good it feels when we use it, than with how efficiently it supports our intended activity. Thus, the most comfortable chair for watching TV may be very inconvenient when working at a computer station, and the latter might not be the best for playing card games.

For example, many homes in the U.S. have chosen to use the high stools and counter tops that would be most comfortable in a bar when having drinks with strangers to replace regular chairs and tables for the family meals. And then we wonder why families don't eat together anymore?

The science of Ergonomics studies the activities of people and looks for better ways of adapting the environment to the person. Today, many pieces of furniture claim to be "ergonomic" especially when describing computer chairs and desks. However, what may be ergonomic for a tall bulky man may not be adequate for a child of school age. So always test furniture before buying it. Try to reproduce ordinary activities that you would perform on that piece of furniture. For example, when choosing a couch, pretend that you are leaning backwards watching TV, that you are leaning forward to have coffee, that you are sitting sideways with your knees bent talking to a friend, etc. When choosing a computer desk and chair, pretend that you are typing, playing video games or browsing the internet while taking notes, or working on a paper for school, etc. Check that there is enough room for your peripherals (printer, scanner, digital camera, etc.) and office supplies (paper, stapler, spare ink cartridges, binders, pens, etc.)

The best test for the comfort of furniture is to listen to your body after performing an activity: Are there any sores or pains? Do you feel numb? Are things too high or too low? Does anything feel out of your reach?

9.2 SAFETY

Anything that is potentially dangerous to a toddler is a threat to an adult's safety too. When there is furniture that is unstable, has sharp edges, protruding legs, or spiky ornaments, the sense of safety is reduced. This includes rugs where people could slide or trip, coffee tables with sharp angles, staircases in poor condition or with no railings, and slippery floors.

Chairs that make us slouch may in time cause back problems. Computer keyboards that are too high may cause metacarpal syndrome (a degenerative condition of hands, wrists and forearms). Computer monitors, TVs and other devices such as microwaves emit energies that are disruptive of natural chi in general and specifically of people's chi (though the new flatscreens have reduced emissions).

Live plants, pets and water fountains or aquariums help restore healthy chi to an environment.

9.3 CONTROL

One of our bigger sources of feeling in control in a room is the ability to see all of it at a glance, especially, being able to see the door.

People who have experienced extreme situations of danger, like veterans of war, instinctively choose the power position for sitting or sleeping. This is the place from which you can see the door but are not sitting or laying right in front of it. In case of an ambush, this position gives the person the vantage point.

While most of us have not experienced warlike conditions, we have all been ambushed in some way or another. It may have been through a sibling that enjoyed tiptoeing behind our backs and going "Booooh!"... or being startled by a newcomer when concentrated at work. Though this may seem like minor issues to our conscious selves, our unconscious minds regard them seriously, therefore an unencumbered view of the door and of most of the room is essential to feeling that we are in control of a physical space.

Another important factor is the ability to reach. The devices, objects, books and other supplies that we use the most in a certain room should be readily available and placed at a height no lower than our knees and no higher than our elbows when we stretch our arms up high, while we can place the items we use less often in high cabinets or low drawers.

9.4 THE POWER POSITION

In Feng Shui we always recommend that people sleep, work and sit in the power position. From the power position, a person has the command of the room, a solid background behind them, a clear view of the entrance, a location that is not in the path of the door.

Lets analyze these requirements one by one:

9.4.1 THE COMMAND OF THE ROOM

Having the command of the room means that from the sitting or lying down position a person needs to be able to see most of the room. If a desk is placed against a wall, for example, this places a person in a disempowered position, because their chair faces a wall and the person's back is exposed to the rest of the room. By switching the desk and chair position and turning them around, the person gets the command of the room.

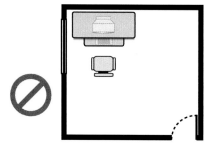
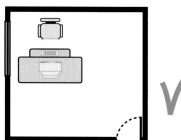

9.4.2 A SOLID BACKGROUND

Most people feel more comfortable when they have a solid wall or a high piece of furniture behind them, to provide back support. There is always a temperature difference between the glass of a window and the surface of a wall and this produces mini-drafts even when windows are perfectly insulated. It is especially important to have a solid wall behind the bed.

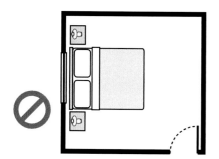 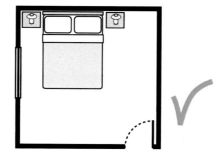

9.4.3 A CLEAR VIEW OF THE ENTRANCE

A clear view of the entrance from the working or reading chair or the bed gives you an added feeling of control.

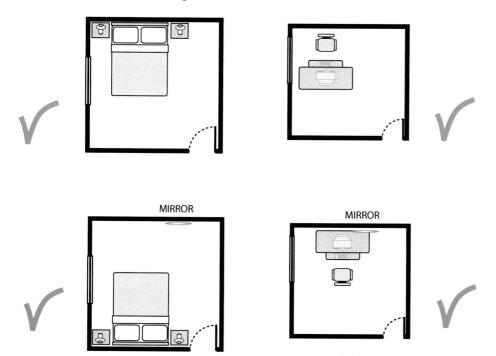

When it is not viable to place the bed or chair in the power position, a mirror can be placed that will allow a view of the door while laying down or sitting at a work station.

9.4.4 NOT BEING IN THE PATH OF THE DOOR

Imagine that you stand at the door of a room with a rolled red rug runner that is exactly the width of the door and unroll it towards the inside all the way to the wall opposite the door. This is the "chi red zone," or the area of the room that is hit by the strong current of chi as it comes in the door, and before it gets gently re-distributed to the rest of the room.

This energy is too fast and strong and therefore it causes problems. No portion of the bed should be overlapping this red zone. No chairs that are used for extended periods of time should be placed in the red zone.

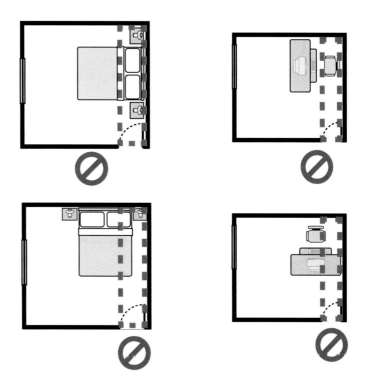

In the four examples above the bed or chair are placed in very disadvantageous positions, in the path of chi. It is best to move them.

However, if it is not possible to move them, you can place a 40 mm faceted crystal ball in between the door and the bed or chair and desk and to try to add some physical block.

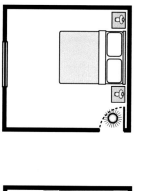
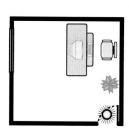
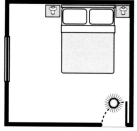
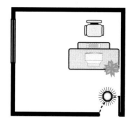

40 mm faceted crystal ball hanging from the ceiling. Traditionally a red string or ribbon is used to signify the protection from the fiery love from heaven, but you can also use fishing line if you want it to be less noticeable. In an office, if there is enough room, you can place a physical barrier, like a plant. Plants are not recommended in bedrooms but I have seen low bookcases effectively used to ameliorate this condition.

9.4.5 NO POSSIBLE GOOD POSITION IN A ROOM

Sometimes I find rooms that were built in such a way that it is impossible to have the bed in the power position. For example, in the graphic below one wall has a closet along its whole length, except for the door opening. Another wall has the door to a bathroom and the two other walls have windows on them.

If you have no choice but to put the headboard against a window, make sure that first you have a headboard and that this headboard is solid (has no cutouts) and is made of wood. A high headboard is better. Have two layers of window treatments, like a rolling blind and heavy curtains. During the winter insulate this window to avoid drafts.

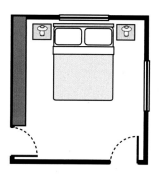

Mirrors in bedrooms can affect the quality of sleep, as chi bounces from smooth surfaces. If sleep is an issue, cover all mirrors with a piece of cloth at night.

NEVER place a mirror on the wall across from the headboard of a bed. This is considered very inauspicious in Feng Shui, and is believed to be a threat to health.

In practical terms, if you woke up and sat up in the bed in the middle of the night, you might startle yourself by seeing your own image in the mirror, thinking it is someone else.

In addition to that, your first view of yourself in the mornings would be of a disheveled you!

129

9.5 Other Feng Shui "Dos and Don'ts" of Furniture Placement

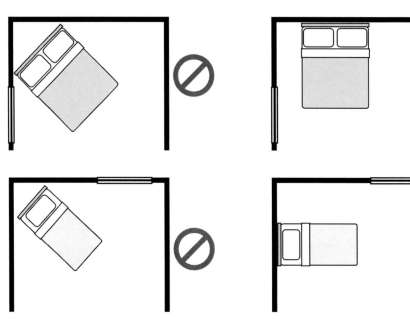

DON'T place the bed with the headboard pointing towards the corner. This position does not provide back support and creates an area of stagnation behind it.

DO place the headboard against a solid wall.

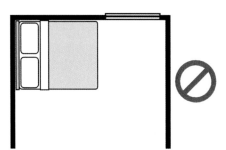

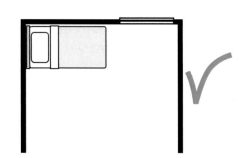

DON'T place a couple's bed with one side against the wall. This blocks the accessibility for the partner that sleeps on that side of the bed. For single people, it symbolically blocks the way for a potential romantic partner.

DO place a child's bed with one side against a solid wall (not against a window), this gives them an added feeling of security and makes falling off the bed less likely. This can also discourage love partnerships before a teen is ready for them.

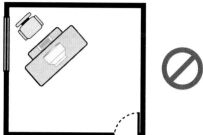
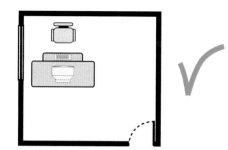

DON'T place a desk and chair in the diagonal position. This furniture placement may make it very hard for a person to concentrate.

DO place a desk and chair parallel to the walls. This gives you a feeling of stability.

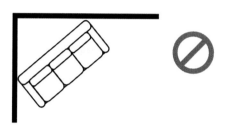
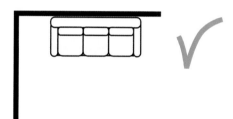

DON'T place a couch at an angle.

DO place a couch parallel to the walls. it is better to have a solid wall but having a window behind it is OK too. You can also place a couch a few feet away from the walls, as long as it is parallel to the walls.

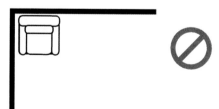
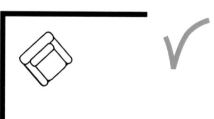

DON'T place a one-person chair with one side against the wall.

DO place a one person chair at an angle. It adds dynamism to a living or family room.

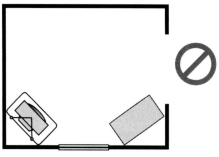

DON'T place large, bulky furniture that was not designed to be in a corner caddy-cornered.

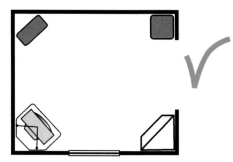

DO place furniture that was designed for corners in corners, as well as small and low square or rectangular pieces of furniture, which may be placed parallel to the walls or at an angle.

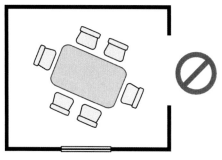

DON'T place large rectangular or oval dining tables at an angle.

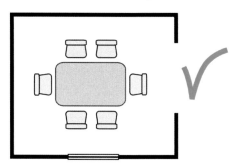

DO place large dining tables parallel to the walls.

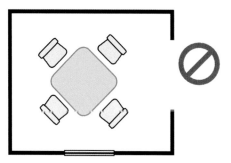

DON'T place square tables in a diamond shape in relation to the walls.

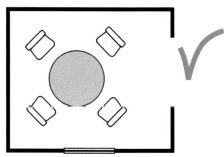

DO place the chairs around a round table at a diagonal.

I hope you have enjoyed reading this book and that you are already implementing some of the life-changing tools I have shared with you for your home.

I look forward to hearing of your successes as you use this system.

You may review this book on Amazon.com and/or contact me at : moni@fengshuiforus.com

When you have experienced the blessings of harmony and prosperity in your home as a result of your application of the knowledge in this text and are ready for more, consider the texts on page 135 to continue your journey down the path of a happy and productive life with Feng Shui.

And if you yearn for an even deeper understanding of Feng Shui, please consider taking the Nine Steps to Feng Shui® Online Course.

Please visit my website www.ninestepstofengshui.com

Many Blessings,

Moni

Moni
Feng Shui Consultant
and Teacher

(865) 973-1475

Moni Castaneda is a Feng Shui consultant, teacher and public speaker, who has been practicing the art of space arrangement for over fifteen years.

Moni has written five text books on Feng Shui: *Feng Shui for Us: The Art of Space Arrangement, Feng Shui Your Own Home, Feng Shui Your Own Life Areas, Feng Shui Your Own Yard, Declutter Your Own Spaces,* and *Feng Shui for Business.* Moni obtained her degree as an architect in Ecuador. Upon moving to the United States she devoted over a decade to study and research Feng Shui.

Moni is the founder of Feng Shui for Us™ and developer of the Nine Steps to Feng Shui® System. The most common feedback Moni gets from students and clients who use her services, have taken her classes, or read her books is: "I feel more hopeful and confident about my life and my future. I know now I have a say in what happens next."

Moni's school of Feng Shui is based on the principles of Traditional Chinese Medicine. Moni offers Feng Shui Online Training Courses on her site. **feng-shui-for-us.teachable.com**

Moni offers online Feng Shui classes, both for people seeking to make Feng Shui a career as consultants, and for those who just want to learn for their own pleasure.

BEFORE THEY START THEIR STUDIES WITH ME, MOST STUDENTS TELL ME THAT THEY ARE CONFUSED. THEY HAVE TRIED TO APPLY FENG SHUI ON THEIR OWN, BUT GOT STUCK WITH SOME QUESTION, OR THEIR CURES DID NOT PRODUCE THE EXPECTED RESULTS.

AFTER THEY TAKE THE NINE STEPS TO FENG SHUI® ONLINE COURSE THIS IS WHAT THEY SAY:

The content was very informative and easy to understand. I feel that I can go into a home or business and practice the Nine Steps System with ease and grace.

Moni was a great instructor, being a teacher myself I know the importance of conveying information in an effective way and not making the student feel "silly" for asking a question. Moni answered all of my questions quickly and she made me feel excited about Feng Shui.

The videos were clear and detailed and were posted in a timely manner so that the course "flowed" and there weren't any interruptions because you could refer back to the manuals and charts that were included in the course. I have previously read many books about feng shui but I was always confused about doing it as a profession because of the conflicting information out there.

Moni brings a fresh perspective that is both holistic and healing and she teaches it from a love paradigm which is absolutely awesome!

Tatia Biddle, Milwaukee, WI

The Nine Steps to Feng Shui® Online Course makes small changes. It also explains concepts that I never learned from other Feng Shui books or practitioners, so the small changes have a big impact.

I wholeheartedly endorse the Nine Steps to Feng Shui® Online Course for anyone that wants to gain a greater understanding of a complex and fascinating art.

Lynda Concord, Knoxville, TN

Thank you so much for offering your Nine Steps to Feng Shui® Online Course. It is so much easier to learn about Feng Shui and work on the things I have learned, one step at a time. I am so grateful that I found your site. You make it simple and easy to understand. I like being able to review the prior videos as well.

Robin R., Montana

Feng Shui Your Own Yard
Easy Landscaping for
Your Home or Business

Feng Shui Your Own Life Areas
Room by Room

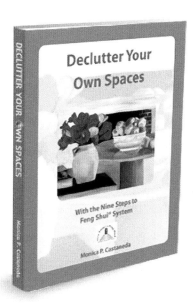

Declutter Your Own Spaces
with the 9 Steps to
Feng Shui® System

Feng Shui Your Own Business
with the 9 Steps to
Feng Shui® System

http://www.ninestepstofengshui.com/feng-shui-books/

Our lives shape our homes. Our homes shape our lives.

Many people don't like the way their home looks and feels. No matter how hard they try, they can't get it right.

They don't realize that when they are arranging their homes, a myriad of memories and emotions come to the surface. As they make their decisions, they need to sort out those memories and choose what's best for them in the now.

This book will help them turn their current homes into dream homes where they can dream their dream lives and realize their full potential by applying Feng Shui secrets for creating a happy home.

The results: a home they can feel proud of, less stress, more vitality and increased wealth, hope and happiness.

Room by Room reveals ancient Feng Shui secrets to live a healthy, abundant, and fulfilled life, through the intimate stories of three homes and four generations, as shared by renowned Feng Shui expert Moni Castaneda.

This book explains how she healed her life, room by room, and how you can too.

http://www.ninestepstofengshui.com/feng-shui-books/

Made in the USA
Middletown, DE
30 November 2021

53899888R00077